CHINA
UNDER COMMUNISM

CHINA
UNDER COMMUNISM
MICHAEL G. KORT

THE MILLBROOK PRESS
BROOKFIELD, CONNECTICUT

Photographs courtesy of Photo Researchers: pp. 12 (© Susan
McCartney), 19 (© Lowell Georgia), 21 (© Simon Fraser), 127
(© Paolo Koch), 157 (© Lynn Lennon); New York Public Library
Picture Collection: p. 15; North Wind Picture Archives: pp. 23,
31; Bettmann: pp. 35, 39, 47, 73, 120, 131, 146; Sovfoto/Eastfoto:
pp. 56, 62, 83, 98; AP/Wide World: pp. 80, 109, 137, 151.
Map by Frank Senyk.

Library of Congress Cataloging-in-Publication Data
Kort, Michael, 1944–
China under communism / Michael G. Kort.
p.   cm.
Includes bibliographical references and index.
Summary: this history of modern China covers the
origins, founding, and development of the country's Communist
regime and examines the forces that are
pushing the country—nuclear power and the home of
a fifth of the world's population—toward change.
ISBN 1-56294-450-9 (lib. bdg.)
1. China—History—1949–   —Juvenile literature [1. China—
History—1949–] I. Title.
DS777.55.K656   1994   951.05—dc 20   94-8312   CIP   AC

Published by The Millbrook Press
2 Old New Milford Road, Brookfield, Connecticut 06804

CONTENTS

For Rick

INTRODUCTION

On October 1, 1949, a peasant-born Communist revolutionary named Mao Zedong stood on a platform facing a gigantic square known as the Gate of Heavenly Peace, or Tiananmen Square, in the city of Beijing. Mao stared out at a huge crowd of more than 200,000 people. Beyond the square and the crowd, the world's most populous country was shuddering in the final throes of civil war. Armies were still fighting, refugees were still fleeing for safety, the starving and the sick were still dying. However, the result was no longer in doubt: The Chinese Communist party under Mao's leadership had won the civil war. Mao's task on October 1 was to announce the founding of the People's Republic of China.

China had changed governments before in its 4,000-year history. But never before had a government come to power determined to rebuild China from the ground up. The founding of the People's Republic was a statement of precisely such an intention. It also was an announcement that a country battered and bled by decades of turmoil, war, and civil conflict would not be allowed to rest. At the same time, it was a declaration that a country that had seen little but despair and trouble for so long finally could hope for a better future.

What happened to China's Communist revolution? In what way did it change the lives of the Chinese people? What price did they pay in the struggle to build a society in which everyone supposedly would be equal? What type of society does China have today? These questions and others about one of the boldest and most ambitious social experiments in history are the focus of this book.

THE CHINESE
EMPIRE

The ancient Chinese proudly called their country the "Middle Kingdom." While the term may have in part reflected how the Chinese understood geography, it was also their statement about China's importance in the world. The Chinese believed that their Middle Kingdom was the center of the civilized universe, which became less civilized and more barbarian the farther one wandered from China. China's legends told how its earliest emperors taught the human race about everything from fire, hunting, and agriculture to writing and musical instruments. The emperor himself was the "Son of Heaven," and he ruled "everything under heaven." In short, the Chinese claimed that they had created human civilization and that their culture was superior to any other.

This self-promoting mythology was for the most part unnecessary, for China's actual history and achievements are impressive enough to stand on their

A monument to the skills of early Chinese engineers,
the Grand Canal has played an important role in
transportation since the early 600s A.D.

own. To be sure, China is not, as its mythology claims, the world's oldest civilization. Civilized life began in the river valleys of Mesopotamia, Egypt, and India a thousand years before it developed along the banks of China's Yellow River. But only the Chinese can claim an unbroken line of four thousand years of one continuous civilization in the same place, extending from the Bronze Age to the Space Age. The unified state they forged in 221 B.C., despite periods of disunity and foreign conquest, still survives. The early mastery of water control and irrigation techniques enabled Chinese farmers to grow enough food to support the largest population of human beings in the world. The Chinese system of writing, while less efficient than other systems that developed later, nonetheless spread across East Asia and remains in use today. It became the vehicle for a literary tradition of prose, poetry, drama, history, and philosophy so rich and prolific that half of all the books in the world before 1750 were written in Chinese. The Chinese called their four basic writing tools—paper, brush, ink, and inkstone—the "four treasures." China's deep respect for learning was summed up by Confucius, the most influential thinker in the country's long history:

> Love of humanity without love of learning soon becomes silliness. Love of wisdom without love of learning soon becomes lack of principle. Love of rectitude without love of learning soon becomes harshness. Love of courage without learning soon becomes chaos.[1]

1. Quoted in Arthur Cotterell, *China: A Cultural History* (New York: New American Library, 1988), p. 71.

Chinese civilization appreciated the world of beauty as well as the world of ideas. Its calligraphy and landscape painting were part of a remarkable artistic heritage, as were the magnificent bronzes of its ancient Shang dynasty. The Chinese were also unusually skilled in combining art and function, the best-known example being their porcelain. Chinese porcelain was the standard of the world for so long that porcelain is simply known as "china," even when it is made in another country. Hardly less famous were China's silks, which provided the rich throughout the ancient world with the delicate and decorative clothing and tapestries they admired and cherished. Chinese silk was in such demand and was so important in international commerce that the ancient trade route known as the "Silk Road" extended across Central Asia and over the centuries linked China and the West.

In terms of technology, the Chinese are probably best known for, and proudest of, what they call the "four inventions": paper, printing, the magnetic compass, and gunpowder. But their technological achievements extend much farther. The modern horse collar (vital for transportation and agriculture), the watertight ship compartment, canal locks, suspension and segmented bridges, the crossbow, and the modest but ever useful wheelbarrow are also Chinese inventions. The Chinese were casting iron and making steel centuries before those processes reached Europe. The 4,000-mile-long (6,400-kilometer) Great Wall and the 1,000-mile-long (1,600-kilometer) Grand Canal are monuments to engineering skills that matched any in the ancient or medieval world. Astronauts report that the Great Wall—begun in the second century B.C. and expanded and rebuilt over many generations to keep

Nineteenth-century Western travelers were impressed by China's Great Wall, shown here in an engraving from 1850.

the nomad horsemen to the north out of China— remains to this day the only human structure visible to the naked eye from space. And until the nineteenth century, Chinese medicine matched anything available elsewhere in the world.

Science was another area in which the Chinese excelled. Chinese astronomy dates from 1300 B.C. Although Chinese astronomers are best known for their observations of the Crab Nebula supernova in A.D. 1054, they also spent centuries studying sunspots and mapping stars. Their mathematical contributions include coordinate geometry and the ancient world's most accurate computation of pi. And it was Chinese alchemy, blended with a dose of primitive chemistry, that led to the invention of gunpowder. After the seventeenth century, when European thinkers developed the scientific method, scientific leadership passed to the West. Western science and technology were central to the development of the modern industrialized world. But for a remarkably long period of about 700 years, from approximately A.D. 700 to 1400, China was the most technologically advanced civilization in the world.

The Chinese Land and People

China is a huge country, the third largest in the world. Its area of almost 3.7 million square miles (9.6 million square kilometers) is exceeded only by those of Russia and Canada, and is slightly more than that of the United States. The Chinese, or Han Chinese, as they are formally called, account for about 95 percent of China's current population. However, the territory they have traditionally occupied, known as China proper, consists of only about 1.5 million square miles (3.9 million square kilometers) in the eastern and southern parts of the country. China proper is divided into four major geographic regions: the North China Plain, drained by the Yellow River; the upper course of the Yangtze (Chang-jiang) River; the lower course of the Yangtze; and the southern coastal region drained by the West River and its tributaries.

The Yellow River valley, in the northern part of China proper, is the ancestral home of the Chinese

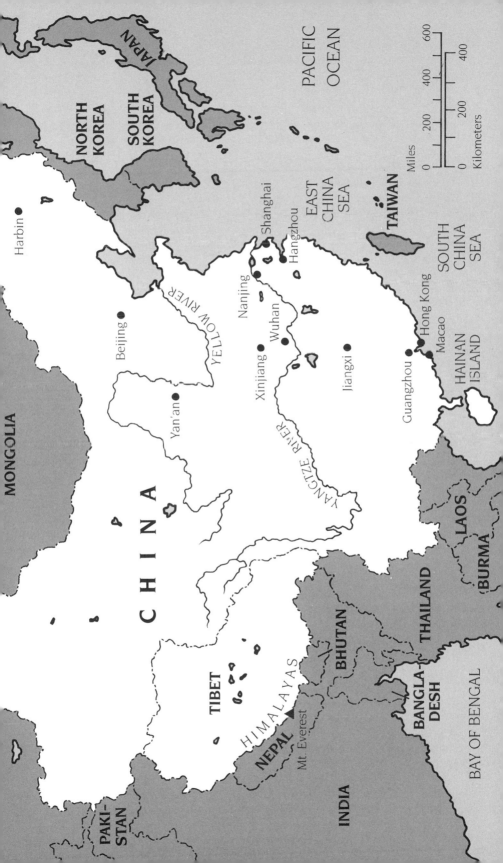

people. The region is covered to a depth of 150 feet (46 meters) by fertile soil called loess, which was carried there from inner Asia by enormous storms during the last ice age. Although the Yellow River valley gets only about 20 to 25 inches (51 to 64 centimeters) of rain per year, its fertile and easily worked soil and the waters of the Yellow River made it an ideal spot for Stone Age hunter-gatherers to make the transition to agriculture, as they had done in Mesopotamia and Egypt. However, the Yellow River has always been both a giver and a taker of life. (Its name comes from the color of the easily eroded loess soil floating in its waters.) Over the centuries, as the soil settled to the bottom as sediment, it raised the river bottom, often causing the river to overflow its banks. The devastating floods, which occurred regularly despite the best efforts of generations of Chinese to control the river with canals and dikes, gave the river its second name: China's Sorrow. The name is well deserved—drought and flood together have caused over 1,800 famines in China in the past 1,800 years.

China's second great river is the Yangtze. Midway along its 3,400-mile (5,500-kilometer) course from soaring inland mountains to the East China Sea, the Yangtze flows through spectacular gorges that today are threatened by plans to build the world's largest dam. While the Chinese did not settle the Yangtze River valley until long after their culture had developed in the north, its suitability for growing rice quickly made it the agricultural heart of China. Generations of Chinese have literally moved mountains of earth to create the rice paddies that have produced the two crops per year that feed China's huge population.

It was, in fact, the expansion of that population that pushed Chinese settlers from northern and cen-

A traditional Chinese sailing craft works
its way along the Yellow River.

tral China into the subtropical lands south of the Yangtze Valley. The conquest of what would become the southern part of China proper began in the third century B.C. One ancient Chinese historian described the lure of the humid south:

> Since the land is so rich in edible products, there is no fear of famine, and therefore the people are content to live from day to day. . . . In the regions south of the Yangzi [Yangtze] and Huai rivers no one ever freezes or starves to death.[2]

But the south was already inhabited by a variety of non-Chinese peoples. As has happened on every continent and in every age when technologically advanced settlers confront weaker peoples, the original inhabitants of southern China were overwhelmed. Some were driven into inaccessible mountains, others were gradually assimilated by the more numerous Chinese, and still others were simply wiped out. The cultures that were destroyed ranged from tribal societies to substantial and advanced kingdoms, but to the advancing Chinese they were "treacherous" and "barbarous" and unworthy of a better fate.

Beyond China proper are vast areas that are sparsely inhabited by China's ethnic minorities. In the west is Xizang (Tibet), the 500,000-square-mile (1,295,000-square-kilometer) "roof of the world." Most of this enormous plateau lies over 12,000 feet (3,700 meters) above sea level. It is crowned by the Himalayas, the world's tallest mountain range, which in turn

2. Quoted in Keith Buchanan, Charles P. FitzGerald, and Colin A. Ronan, *China* (New York: Crown Publishers, 1980), p. 59.

The ice-covered north peak of Mt. Everest,
on the Tibetan side of the mountain.

is topped by Mount Everest, the world's highest peak. The Tibetans were once a warlike people capable of resisting the more numerous Chinese. Today, gentled by their Buddhist religion and overwhelmed by the brute force of China's Communist government, their culture is being destroyed and their land flooded by waves of immigration from China proper. In the northwest are the deserts and mountains of Xinjiang, home to six million Turkic-speaking Muslim tribesmen. Directly northward is Mongolia, whose semiarid steppe became the cradle of Ghengis Khan's great empire. In the northeast is Manchuria, a huge expanse of lowlands and wooded mountains blessed with fertile soil and abundant mineral resources. In the seventeenth century, the native Manchus burst out of their homeland to conquer China and rule it for almost three hundred years.

Traditional Chinese Society and Confucianism

China has long been one of the most tightly regulated societies in the world. Ancient China developed in this way because it depended on its ability to control water. In the north, inadequate rainfall meant that survival depended on complex irrigation works, while in the south, growing rice required flooding and then draining the fields for each crop. This in turn required that people work together on a daily basis and that masses of people be mobilized regularly for large water-control projects. These demands produced a way of life very different from modern Western culture, where maximizing individual freedom has been the main goal

This print shows Chinese peasants irrigating rice fields and transplanting seedlings.

of society. In China, the individual was completely subordinated to the group. Each individual was taught his place in society and was required to fulfill it without question. The concepts of individual freedom and democracy, so central to modern Western society, were completely alien to China's values and way of life. Chinese society was a strict hierarchical social pyramid grounded in inequality, with the emperor and a small elite at the top and the masses, or ordinary people, at the bottom.

The family played a key role in preparing people for their places in society and in keeping them there.

The Chinese family was based on the authority of the father. He had almost total control over family members, from his wife, whom he could divorce at will, to his children, whose very lives were often in his hands. Children owed their father what was called "filial piety," a concept of obedience that went far beyond what is customary in modern Western life. For example, Chinese children were told the story of a young man who accidentally hit his father while warding off several attackers. But because filial piety prohibited striking one's father under any circumstances, the unfortunate youth was executed.

Women in China had an especially hard lot. Although her husband could divorce her, a woman's only escape from an unbearable marriage was usually suicide. Women had few property rights, and often had to share their husbands with other wives or with concubines. China's ancient *Book of Songs* shows how differently the Middle Kingdom valued men and women:

> *Sons shall be born to him.*
> *They will be put to sleep on couches;*
> *They will be clothed in robes . . .*
>
> *Daughters shall be born to him.*
> *They will be put to sleep on the ground;*
> *They will be clothed in wrappers. . . .*
>
> *A clever man builds a city;*
> *A clever woman lays one low . . .*
> *For disorder does not come from heaven*
> *But is brought about by women.*[3]

3. Quoted in Hilda Hookham, A *Short History of China* (New York: New American Library, 1972), p. 51.

Beginning in the tenth century, physical injury was added to the lowliness of a woman's place in Chinese life with the crippling custom of foot-binding. Young girls were forced to have their toes bound under the arches of their feet. Because of this, the feet were broken, and as they grew they were deformed, becoming the tiny "lily feet" that were about half normal size and considered a mark of female beauty in China. But for millions of women—over half of all Chinese women by the nineteenth century—beauty and desirability were bought at the price of constant pain and great difficulty in walking.

The philosophic underpinning of Chinese life was called Confucianism. Confucius (551–479 B.C.) was a scholar and teacher who developed and expanded ideas already deeply rooted in Chinese culture before his birth. Confucius was convinced that he knew how to manage society. He commented:

> If some ruler would employ me, in a
> month I would have my system working.
> In three years, everything would be
> running smoothly.[4]

The great scholar never got a chance to prove that statement in his lifetime, but his ideas were central to the way China was run for more than twenty centuries after he died.

The main goal of Confucianism was what the Chinese called a harmonious society. The key to this was to maintain social order. However, Confucianism

---

4. Quoted in John A. Harrison, *The Chinese Empire* (New York and London: Harcourt, Brace, Jovanovich, 1972), p. 53.

taught that social order could not be maintained by force. It required that all persons in China's hierarchical society accept without question their status in life, whether high or low. The central concept in Confucianism for guaranteeing that people accepted their place was *li*, or behavior according to status. Unlike in the West of today, where codes of conduct and law are supposed to apply equally to everyone, in Confucian China each category of people was supposed to behave according to rules appropriate to its place in the social pyramid. Under Confucianism it was proper for a husband to strike a wife, but a wife who struck her husband would be severely punished. *Li* also directed that people be treated according to their social status. Thus the classic texts record that Confucius himself "spoke out boldly" when addressing an inferior, but "spoke respectfully" when addressing a superior. A poem from the ancient *Book of Odes* summed up the Confucian view of behavior:

> *From East and West*
> *From North and South*
> *Came none who thought of disobedience.*[5]

These elaborate rules applied to the upper classes; Confucian tradition relied on strict laws and punishments to control the millions of ordinary Chinese peasants. However, those in power, including the emperor, were expected to deliver good government. This could only be done, Confucianism taught, if they ruled according to Confucian rules and moral teachings. Their virtuous conduct had to serve as an example to

5. Quoted in Orville Shell and Joseph Esherick, *Modern China* (New York: Random House, 1972), p. 2.

others. Only if they behaved according to Confucian standards could China's rulers govern effectively and ensure social order. In other words, China's rulers were expected to deliver good and moral government.

China's Confucian ideal, then, was a government that was a kind of benevolent despotism. But it was still despotism. The law served the state, not the people. Over six hundred crimes were punishable by death, and torture was used to make people confess. For the ordinary Chinese person, it was best to stay out of the government's way.

According to traditions that developed after Confucius's death, the key to proper behavior and hence to knowing how to behave lay in the classic Confucian texts. China therefore developed a unique system for selecting the officials who would serve the emperor and govern his realm. All officials had to pass excruciatingly difficult examinations, a task that required years of study. In theory, the examinations were open to all males, but in practice only the sons of wealthy landowners could afford the tutors and time to prepare for the examinations. The examination system, which began as early as the second century A.D., provided China with a loyal bureaucracy steeped in Confucian values; this probably made ancient and medieval China the best-governed society in the world.

There was one exception to the harsh economic reality that allowed only the sons of wealthy landowners to take the examinations and join China's ruling class. On extremely rare occasions, a village might pool its resources to allow an extraordinarily talented peasant boy to prepare for the exams. If he succeeded—and the odds were against anyone passing these exams—the boy would bring great honor to his village. This needle's eye of opportunity had nothing to do with equal opportunity for China's peasants or with democracy. Almost all Chinese lived and died without the slightest chance of bettering their status. But because the examination system was not restricted to the wealthy it did make China's ruling elite more vibrant and durable than the completely hereditary upper classes of other traditional societies.

At the top of Chinese society stood the all-powerful emperor. Although in theory he ruled according to divine rules, in practice there was little to limit his power. An emperor could, on a whim, destroy the career and even the life of the highest official. One emperor, for example, forced 107 high officials to kneel outside his palace gate for five successive days—and they were more fortunate than other officials who were whipped to death with bamboo poles.

But officials were far better off than the millions of ordinary peasants who spent their entire lives at the mercy of the officials who ruled them. For ordinary Chinese, the state was something to be feared and avoided. The law was not something that protected them, as in modern Western societies, but was a tool the state used to control them. In a society where the collective was more important than the individual, an entire family could be punished, and even executed, for an illegal act committed by one of its members.

The Peak and Decline of Chinese Civilization

China's long history prior to 1911 is divided according to the various dynasties that ruled the country. Between several of the dynasties, there were also periods of disunity that lasted for varying lengths of time. Chinese civilization probably peaked during a five hundred-year period from the seventh to the twelfth century. In the thirteenth century, a foreign power overran the entire country for the first time when the Mongols completed a bitterly resisted, decades-long conquest in 1279. The Mongols were driven from China in 1368 and were replaced by a native dynasty, the Ming. Their defeat in 1644 at the hands of the non-Chinese Manchus marked the second foreign conquest of China. But the victorious Manchus, like other invaders of China in the past, could not challenge Chinese culture. Although they maintained their separate identity until their collapse in 1911, they gradually were assimilated, so that their dynasty—the Qing—is generally considered to be Chinese.

The real threat to China lay not among the hordes of nomadic conquerers stampeding into China from the northern plains, but from tiny groups of merchants and adventurers slowly floating ashore from the southern seas after many months of travel from their distant homes in Western Europe. Small numbers of Europeans could threaten China because they were part of a vibrant civilization whose technology was increasingly leaving the rest of the world, including China, behind. At the same time, by the fifteenth century technological progress in China was stagnating. This was true in virtually every area, from agriculture to military techniques. Several factors account for this. The Confucian tradition stressed memorization, not the critical thinking crucial to the European scientific method that produced the Scientific Revolution in the West. Confucianism also stressed the past, and the formality associated with its ideas had become increasingly restrictive after the rise of the Ming dynasty. Because Confucian thinkers focused on traditional ideas and on the past, they were not equipped to grasp and use the new ideas and techniques that drove scientific and technological progress in Europe.

Another key factor in China's decline was that by the fifteenth century China's huge population was becoming too heavy a weight for its resources to bear. With less to go around per person each year, China over several centuries gradually but unstoppably was transformed from a rich society into a poor one. And just as the Middle Kingdom was facing these dangerous long-term problems, the Europeans came knocking at its door.

China and the West

The Chinese considered themselves superior to foreigners, whom they called "barbarians." Foreign states were expected to accept their inferiority in their dealings with the Middle Kingdom. For centuries before Europeans arrived on its shores, the Chinese Empire dealt with foreign states in Asia through the tribute system. Representatives of other countries were expected to bring tribute to the emperor. When presenting that tribute, they had to perform the kowtow, a series of bows that included touching one's head to the floor and that left no doubt of who enjoyed superior status. Since China was by far the largest and, except in times of disunity, the most powerful state in East Asia, it was able to enforce the tribute system on its neighbors.

When European traders arrived, the Chinese saw no reason to treat them differently than any other

Smoking an opium pipe. Opium, smuggled into China by European merchants, disrupted Chinese society in the early 1800s.

foreigners. Neither the Portuguese, the first to arrive, in 1514, nor the British, whose first ship docked in 1637, nor any other Westerners impressed the Chinese. The Chinese considered the Europeans, who often arrived unwashed after months at sea, as foul-smelling barbarians. One Chinese scholar said of them:

> They all look alike, though differing in height; some being very tall. My present idea of them is ugliness and stiff angular demeanor. . . . Their cheeks are white and hollow, though occasionally purple; their noses like sharp beaks, which we consider unfavor-

able. Some of them have thick tufts of hair, red and yellow, making them look like monkeys. Though sleepy looking, I think they have intelligence.[6]

The Chinese dictated strict rules that European traders had to follow. They could do business only in China's southern port of Guangzhou (Canton). Europeans could trade only with special groups of Chinese merchants, and had to live in restricted areas outside the city. Another frustrating thing for the Europeans was that while they wanted to buy many Chinese products, the Chinese were not interested in European goods. This was especially troublesome for the British, the most active traders in China, who bought huge amounts of Chinese tea and had to pay for them in scarce gold and silver.

Eventually China's growing internal difficulties benefited the Europeans, and especially the British. By the nineteenth century, China's decline had reached an advanced state. It trailed far behind the Europeans in military technology, and its huge population had become a crushing burden. In addition, the Manchu dynasty had grown weak and corrupt, which increased the hardships of the Chinese people. To escape their misery, many of them turned to smoking opium. In defiance of Chinese law, the British and other Westerners in the China trade began to smuggle opium into China. When China tried to stop the trade by seizing British opium, the British declared war on China. After the first Opium War (1839–1842), the victorious British in the Treaty of Nanjing forced China to open up addi-

6. Ibid., p. 21.

tional ports for trade and took control of the island of Hong Kong. The Treaty of Nanjing was only the first of many "unequal treaties" China was forced to sign. Other Western countries quickly made their own demands on China. After the second Opium War, in which France joined Britain against China, the Chinese were forced to legalize the import of opium.

The United States also became involved in China. It signed a treaty with China in 1844 that allowed Americans in China to be governed by United States rather than Chinese law. Far worse for China, between 1858 and 1860 the Russian Empire annexed hundreds of thousands of square miles of China's northern territory. China simply was too weak to stop any of this. The Middle Kingdom, for so long the dominant power in East Asia, had begun a century of humiliation at the hands of foreigners.

The second part of the nineteenth century brought only further grief to China. Between 1850 and 1864 the country was torn apart by a disastrous civil war called the Taiping Rebellion in which 30 million people died. The Taiping rebels won millions of poor Chinese peasants to their side by promising a society based on equality and communal ownership of property. After several years of spectacular success, the movement was defeated, in part because its leadership became totally corrupt, thus making a lie out of its promise of equality. Even so, the Taiping rebels would serve to inspire later Chinese revolutionaries.

The Taiping rebellion was only one of a long series of rebellions that shook China and the Manchu dynasty during the nineteenth century. They were followed by yet another blow at the hands of a foreign country. During 1894–1895, China fought a war with

Japan over Korea, suffering a disastrous defeat. This was especially humiliating for the Chinese, who had long received tribute from the Japanese and looked upon them as inferiors.

China's defeat by Japan cost the Middle Kingdom more than its pride. The victorious Japanese enthusiastically joined other nations in taking advantage of China. They annexed the Chinese island of Formosa (now known as Taiwan), as well as other territory. This loss was followed by what the Chinese called the "carving of the melon," when Britain, France, Germany, and Russia rushed in to carve out what they called "concessions," or spheres of influence, in China. While the concessions were not large areas or colonies in the usual sense, they were important territories along the coast where foreigners could do as they wanted without being subject to Chinese law. This meant that in parts of their own country, Chinese were treated as second-class citizens by the foreign occupiers.

The Chinese responded in 1900 with an anti-foreign uprising called the Boxer Rebellion. The Boxers were mainly peasants and other poor people, such as unemployed laborers. They were called "Boxers" by Europeans in China because the exercises they did seemed to resemble boxing. In 1900 they began attacking and murdering foreigners and the Chinese who associated with them. After some hesitation, the Chinese government supported them. Military forces from Britain, Russia, Germany, Japan, France, Austria, Italy, and the United States put down the Boxer Rebellion after being rushed to China's capital of Beijing.

While all these defeats were taking place, the Chinese made several attempts to introduce reforms that would allow them to modernize and stand up to

These Boxers, members of a great society that opposed Western influences, were imprisoned after their 1900 rebellion was crushed.

the Europeans and Japan. These efforts—during the 1860s and 1870s, in 1898, and in 1905—were complete failures. China's old Confucian system was simply incapable of competing with the modern capitalist West. After the failure of the 1898 reforms, young Chinese intellectuals who had come into contact with Westerners and were fed up with their country's weakness rejected Confucian values in favor of Western ideas. However, they were a minuscule minority in China and could do little to influence events. Then, in 1911, uprisings in several Chinese provinces easily brought down the decaying Manchu dynasty. The uprisings were not a unified movement. They were led by local military men and officials who had concluded that the Manchu dynasty could no longer govern.

With the collapse of the empire, a republic was declared. The old Confucian system, which had dominated Chinese life for over two thousand years, had finally perished. The great challenge for China was to find a new system to take its place.

THE CHINESE REPUBLIC

The English poet Matthew Arnold, although writing about another place in another century, has provided an apt description of China in the decade after 1911:

Wandering between two worlds, one dead,
the other powerless to be born.[1]

The dead world in China was the Confucian era, as most recently represented by the defunct Manchu dynasty. The world unable to be born was a republican form of government that allowed citizens a role in making the decisions that governed their lives. The wanderers were the Chinese people, bewildered by the collapse of their ancient empire and tormented by the turmoil and violence that had replaced it.

1. Matthew Arnold, "Tales from the Grand Chartreuse," *The Poems of Matthew Arnold*, ed. Kenneth Allott (New York: Barnes and Noble, 1965), p. 289.

Sun Yatsen: The Father
of the Chinese Revolution

The man most identified with trying to create a new Chinese world was Sun Yatsen. He was born in 1866 in southern China, where Western influence was strong. However, he was educated and learned English in Hawaii, where his older brother lived. Sun became a physician in Macao, a Portuguese colony near Guangzhou, but from the beginning his medical career became intertwined with politics. In effect, he became China's first professional revolutionary. Sun organized his first political group shortly after returning to China in 1895 and that year attempted the first of at least ten unsuccessful attempts to overthrow the Manchus.

Sun became well known in revolutionary circles for his Three Principles of the People: nationalism, democracy, and an economic program called the "people's livelihood." Nationalism called for expelling the foreign powers and the Manchus from China. Sun's version of democracy was quite different from democracy as it is known in the West. Sun included a period of "tutelage" prior to putting democracy into effect. Also, following Chinese tradition, he gave far more power to the state than do Western democracies. "People's livelihood," Sun's version of socialism, called for state control of much of the economy to promote greater equality in China.

Although Sun had failed to overthrow the Manchus, when the dynasty finally did fall he was selected to be the provisional president of the new Chinese republic on December 29, 1911. He officially took office and declared the establishment of the Republic of

Sun Yatsen, shown with his wife.

China on January 1, 1912. However, President Sun was unable to establish control over any part of China. He therefore sought someone who could, and in the end found Yuan Shikai, the most powerful general in China. Yuan had served the Manchus and had never supported a republic, but Sun and his supporters were desperate. With nothing more than Yuan's promise to support the republic, Sun gave up his lifetime dream and resigned the presidency in favor of Yuan. The general then immediately began to establish a military dictatorship. He also tried to destroy Sun's political party, the Guomindang (GMD) (Kuomintang, or Nationalist party), and even briefly tried to make himself emperor. He died in 1916 after four stormy years in office.

Yuan's death did not make things better. With no military leader powerful enough to maintain order, central authority collapsed. Although it remained a republic officially, in reality China was ruled by military strongmen, or warlords, each of whom controlled a piece of the country. Some warlords tried to govern well, but the period as a whole was a disaster for China. Rival armies crisscrossed the land, killing and looting as they came and went. Warlords drove the peasants to ruin with endless taxes they imposed to finance their petty wars. In one province peasants were paying their taxes ten years in advance even though the region was swept by famine. An eyewitness described what happened to a provincial town when a warlord arrived:

> The arrival . . . was the signal for a general looting of the city. I have never seen more thorough work. Every shop, every house in

the beautiful and prosperous city has been literally stripped. There is not a vestige of any usable commodity from one end of the city to the other. . . . Most of the population has fled. . . .[2]

China's politicians could do nothing to control the warlords. The official government in Beijing had no power; nor did a rival government led by Sun that was set up in Guangzhou.

While warlords went on a rampage inside the country, China faced an outside threat from Japan. The outbreak of World War I distracted the major European powers, who were locked in mortal combat with each other thousands of miles from China. This gave Japan an opportunity to expand its interests. The Japanese declared war on Germany, took over German territory in China, and signed secret agreements with Britain and France to keep that territory when the war was over. Far more dangerous, in 1915 they presented China with the notorious "Twenty-one Demands," which threatened to turn China into a virtual Japanese colony. While the Chinese struggled to keep Japan at bay, they declared war on Germany in 1917, hoping that as a reward German concessions would be returned to Chinese control when the war was over.

Chinese hopes went unfulfilled. In 1919, a year after World War I ended with Germany's defeat, the victorious powers dictated peace terms at the Treaty of Versailles. On May 4, after the news arrived in China that German concessions had been turned over to

2. Quoted in James Sheridan, *China in Disintegration* (New York: The Free Press, 1977), pp. 91–92.

Japan, bitterly angry Chinese reacted with widespread anti-Japanese demonstrations and strikes. These demonstrations were the starting point for what is known as the May 4th Movement. The May 4th Movement has been called China's Renaissance. It drew on ideas that had been circulating for over a decade among young Chinese who had been exposed to Western influences. But the May 4th Movement went much further and involved far more people than what had gone on before. It was an intellectual explosion, a varied and creative outburst of activity involving many thousands of students and intellectuals. It emphasized both a rejection of Confucianism and a patriotic commitment to a new and revitalized China.

The May 4th Movement took many forms, from personal to intellectual to political. Students rejected traditional arranged marriages and looked for marriage partners on the basis of "love and romance." Young women moved beyond the traditional limits placed on them and began to seek an education and socialize with men as Western women did. Intellectuals refused to write in classical Chinese, which only a few people could understand, and began writing in the spoken language of the day. They started publishing hundreds of new journals and magazines with names like *New China* and *The New Man*. Among them were Chen Duxiu, who had begun publishing his magazine *New Youth* back in 1915. Other leading intellectuals were Hu Shi, who led the fight for literature written in spoken Chinese, and Lu Xun, who is considered to be China's finest modern writer. Participants in the May 4th Movement often discussed political ideas, including Western democratic principles. At the same time, some Chinese intellectuals, feeling betrayed by the

West, rejected Western democratic and capitalist ideas.

Some of those looking for new answers to China's problems found them in a doctrine called Marxism. Based on the ideas of Karl Marx, a nineteenth-century German philosopher, Marxism claimed that capitalism was a doomed system that would be succeeded by socialism. Under socialism, the capitalist free-market system would be replaced by a planned economy, and the economic inequality of capitalism would be replaced by equality. There would be no rich and no poor; instead, planning and fairness would provide enough for everyone to live well. Of course, socialism could not just happen. It would require a violent revolution to overthrow the capitalists and their system. That revolution would be made by the industrial workers, or proletariat, who made up the majority of the population in modern capitalist societies. Society would pass through a stage called socialism, during which the old habits and inequalities of capitalism would be dissolved, and would then proceed to communism, where perfect equality would reign. The governing principle would be, said Marx, "From each according to his ability, to each according to his needs."

Karl Marx died in 1883 before a successful socialist revolution could take place. However, in 1917 a Marxist party called the Bolsheviks seized power in Russia, the largest country in the world. Inspired by that victory, in 1921 two Marxists, Chen Duxiu and Li Dazhao, organized the Chinese Communist party (CCP). The founding meeting, which began in a girls' boarding school in the port city of Shanghai and finished, after a police raid, on a houseboat near the city of Hangzhou, was attended by twelve delegates. One of them was Mao Zedong (Mao Tse-tung), a young peasant from Hunan province.

The CCP was founded with the help of the Soviet Union, the new name the Bolsheviks gave to the former Russian Empire. Like all Communist parties, the CCP took its orders from the Soviet leadership through a Soviet-controlled organization called the Communist International, or Comintern. Two years later, the Comintern ordered the CCP to form an alliance with another struggling party, Sun Yatsen's Guomindang. Sun had agreed to the alliance because he would get Soviet help in organizing his party and building up an army. The Soviets wanted the alliance because they reasoned that if China were strong enough to expel the European powers, this would weaken them and would speed up communist revolutions in Europe. As a result, a partnership called the First United Front was forged in 1923. Sun finally got the support he desperately needed, but he did not live to enjoy it. He died of cancer in 1925.

Chiang Kai-shek and the Establishment of Nationalist China

Sun Yatsen was succeeded by a soldier, Chiang Kaishek (1887–1975). The son of a merchant, Chiang began his military career at the age of twenty. Beginning in 1915, he served Sun Yatsen as a military adviser. In 1923, Sun sent Chiang to study military affairs in Moscow. His course completed, Chiang returned home with a deep mistrust of the Communists. Chiang, in fact, was a conservative who did not want to see real social change in China. He had the support of conservative bankers, businessmen, and landlords. None of these people was pleased to see Communist party members working within the GMD organizing peasants and the small but growing urban working class. The GMD conservatives wanted stability in China so they could maintain their positions, not a socialist revolution—the goal of the CCP—which would take from them everything they had.

In Chiang Kai-shek the conservative wing of the GMD found the man it needed. In 1926, Chiang launched his "Northern Expedition" from Guang-zhou, the GMD's base in southern China. The goal was to seize warlord territory and reunify China under a central government controlled by the GMD. Chiang was aided in his effort by his Soviet advisers and his CCP allies, who organized both peasants in the coun-tryside and workers in the city to support GMD forces against the warlords.

During 1926 and early 1927, large areas fell to Chiang's troops, including several major cities. In late March 1927, his troops entered Shanghai, the teeming and bustling port city near the mouth of the Yangtze River and China's most important commercial center. The Guomindang took the city without a fight, because Communist-led labor unions had seized control there and welcomed what they thought were their GMD al-lies. But they were terribly wrong. In mid-April, Chiang turned on the Communists, launching what became known as the White Terror. Thousands of Communists were rounded up and shot, both in Shanghai and else-where in China. Only the very fortunate managed to escape. These survivors included Mao Zedong, the CCP's future leader, and Zhou Enlai (Chou En-lai), for many years the party's second most important figure. During the White Terror, Chiang announced the establishment of a new Nationalist government in Nanjing, a city on the Yangtze about 200 miles (320 kilometers) inland from Shanghai. When the CCP tried to respond with uprisings against the Guomindang in the fall and winter of 1927, its weakened forces were totally defeated.

Chiang's conquests continued into 1928 and brought greater unity to China than at any time since the death of the military dictator Yuan Shikai. Through persistent negotiations, Chiang also reduced the areas of European control in China, recovering control of twenty of the thirty-six European concessions in his country. The Nationalist regime also made some progress in modernizing China between the late 1920s and mid-1930s. Railroads and new roads were built, and postal and telegraph services were improved. Secondary education expanded by four times, and the number of college students studying the sciences and technical subjects doubled. At the same time, currency reform promoted economic stability. Industrial growth was impressive, although modern industry remained a tiny fraction of China's overall economy. In addition, China's most modern industries, railroads, and mines remained largely in foreign hands.

Chiang also scored another victory over the Communists, some of whom had managed to regroup in remote areas of the countryside. The most successful CCP group, which was led by Mao, controlled a small area in the mountains of southern China that Mao called the "Chinese Soviet Republic." After failing to dislodge the Communists in four "extermination" campaigns, Chiang began a fifth campaign in 1934, aided this time by advisers from Nazi Germany. By the spring of 1934, the Communist forces were defeated and on the run, the "Chinese Soviet Republic" destroyed.

Chiang Kai-shek.

Chiang's problem was that the failings of his Nationalist regime far outweighed its successes. For one thing, Chiang never defeated many of China's warlords; instead, he made arrangements in which they agreed to accept his authority but remained in control of their fiefdoms. The warlords proved to be unreliable allies, and by 1936 there had been over twenty uprisings against his government. Far more dangerous than any warlord or group of warlords were the Japanese. In 1931 they seized Manchuria, a huge and rich region in northern China, and turned it into a puppet kingdom they called Manchukuo. With powerful forces in Manchuria, the Japanese constantly threatened to expand farther into China.

Another shortcoming of the Nationalist regime was the nature of the Guomindang itself. When Chiang purged the Communists from the GMD, he drove out the very people who had reached out to China's masses, both its industrial working class and its peasantry. The Communists were the ones who had been making a serious attempt to fulfill the "people's livelihood" principle of Sun Yatsen's program. With them gone, the GMD increasingly based itself on conservative social classes: the banking and merchant interests in the cities and the landlords in the countryside. Unions and other workers' organizations were suppressed. Peasants were charged backbreaking rents because a 1930 law limiting rents to 37.5 percent of the crop was ignored. The people who benefited most from GMD policies were the bankers who financed the regime and who were linked to Chiang through personal ties.

Chiang also had ties to China's underworld. During the White Terror, he received help from Shanghai's notorious criminal "Green Gang." His most important base of support, however, was the army. By the mid-1930s army personnel made up over 40 percent of the GMD leadership. So it was not surprising that in any given year military expenses absorbed at least half the government's revenue. Much of the rest went to pay the GMD regime's growing debt, leaving very little to deal with China's massive social and economic problems. Meanwhile, the Nationalist regime grew increasingly corrupt. Officials took advantage of the lack of supervision from above to supplement their salaries through graft. Instead of providing public service, many government employees followed the slogan "Become an official and get rich."

Those Chinese who disapproved of the Nationalist regime did so at great risk. By the 1930s, Chiang had tossed out Sun Yatsen's commitment to democracy in favor of fascism. He admired both Benito Mussolini of Italy and Adolf Hitler of Germany, its two main practitioners. Chiang believed that a fascist dictatorship would give China the order and strength he insisted it needed. As he put it:

> In fascism, the organization, the spirit, and the activities must all be militarized. . . . In the home, the factory, the government office, everyone's activities must be the same as in the army. . . . In other words, there must be obedience, sacrifice, strictness, cleanliness, accuracy, diligence, secrecy. . . . And everyone must firmly and bravely sacrifice for the group and nation.[3]

3. Quoted in Lloyd Eastman, "Nationalist China during the Nanking Decade," *The Cambridge History of China*, vol. 13, John King Fairbank and Albert Feuerwerker, ed. (Cambridge, London, and New York: Cambridge University Press, 1986), pp. 125–126.

Those who disagreed with Chiang became the target of GMD gangs called the Blue Shirts, who were modeled on Hitler's Brown Shirts and Mussolini's Black Shirts. In short, by the mid-1930s, the Guomindang regime had become a dictatorship that opposed reforms and enriched its leadership while China's problems festered and grew worse. Still, the Guomindang had a firm grip on China, and Chiang Kai-shek stood unchallenged as the country's president and leader.

Mao Zedong and the Chinese Communist Party

The first task for the survivors of the disaster of 1927 was to figure out what had gone wrong. Prior to 1928, the CCP had followed traditional Marxist strategy while taking its orders from the Soviet Union. Unfortunately, neither traditional Marxism nor Soviet instructions were helpful guides for political success in China.

Traditional Marxism said the industrial working class—the proletariat—was the class that would make the socialist revolution. That in turn required that Marxist parties focus most of their attention on that class. But in China the industrial workers made up less than 1 percent of the population, while the peasantry, which traditional Marxism largely ignored, made up over 90 percent. Traditional Marxism assumed that peasants were too backward and ignorant to ever make a socialist revolution. Soviet instructions therefore stressed Marxism's emphasis on the industrial workers in the cities at the expense of the peasants. They also reflected political disputes in Moscow and had little to do with the realities in China. Nonetheless, the CCP leadership faithfully followed those instructions. Because of Soviet instructions to form the First United Front, the CCP was helpless and unprepared in 1927 when Chiang turned his guns against its members, a fact that was not lost on several surviving CCP leaders, including Mao Zedong.

Mao was born in 1893 into a prosperous peasant family in Hunan province, a rice-growing region in the interior of China. He defied his father's wishes that he just work on the family farm and insisted on getting a primary school education. He participated in the uprisings of 1911 and entered Beijing University in 1918, where Li Dazhao, soon to be the cofounder of the CCP, was head librarian. During the First United Front with the GMD, Mao went outside the traditional Marxist mold and worked on organizing peasants rather than workers. In 1927 he issued a report in which he predicted that the socialist revolution Marxists were working for would be carried out by the peasants:

> In a very short time, in China's central, southern, and northern provinces, several hundred million peasants will rise like a mighty storm, like a hurricane, a force so swift and violent that no power, however great, will be able to hold it back. They will smash all the trammels that bind them and rush forward along the road to liberation. They will sweep all the imperialists, warlords, corrupt officials, local tyrants and evil gentry into their graves.[4]

4. Mao Zedong, "Report on an Investigation of the Peasant Movement in Hunan, March 1927," in Vera Simone, ed., *China in Revolution: History, Documents, and Analyses* (New York: Fawcett, 1968), p. 179.

Mao's bold and ferocious prediction proved to be premature, in part because Chiang threw his own lightning bolts at the CCP before any peasant storm could rise. After Chiang's White Terror shattered the bulk of the CCP in the spring of 1927, Mao followed party orders and led a doomed uprising in the autumn. After narrowly escaping with his life, Mao retreated to a remote mountain region in Jiangxi Province in southern China, there to begin to rebuild a new Chinese Communist party.

The Jiangxi period lasted from 1928 to 1934. While working and living with a small group of followers in virtual isolation, Mao for several years had the advantage of being free from interference from both Moscow and the CCP leaders who followed Soviet orders. Gradually, Mao developed his own strategy for making a socialist revolution in China. The first principle required a radical change in Marxist ideology. In China, Mao insisted, the rural peasantry, not the urban proletariat, would make the socialist revolution. This assertion got Mao into trouble with the CCP leadership, and Mao found himself compelled to make verbal concessions to traditional Marxist thinking. For example, when Mao announced the founding of the Chinese Soviet Republic in 1931 in Jiangxi, he and his followers had to write laws favoring the local proletariat. In fact, there was no proletariat in rural and remote Jiangxi province. But the law was written because in theory Marxists should work with that class. In practice, Mao put all his efforts into organizing the local peasants and building his party organization on them.

A second Maoist principle, painfully learned in 1927, was that the party had to be protected by its own army. But that was not enough. The Communist party's army had to be radically different from the warlord or GMD armies, which preyed on the people by looting, raping, and killing rather than protecting. Mao and his top military leader, a former GMD soldier named Zhu De, began to build an army that the peasants not only would not fear but would want to help. That help, in fact, was crucial, for without it CCP forces could not survive against the far more powerful GMD army. The CCP's army, which was called the Red Army, had to use hit-and-run guerrilla tactics against the GMD. Its soldiers could do that only if the peasants willingly helped them—so treating the peasants well was both correct from a revolutionary point of view and essential from a military one.

The Red Army, which after 1946 was called the People's Liberation Army (PLA), therefore followed strict rules. Peasants were to be well treated, army units were to pay for what they needed, and individual soldiers who stayed in peasants' homes were to behave politely and clean up after themselves. Mao and Zhu did not miss many details. They even required their soldiers to dig latrines "at a safe distance from people's houses" and, at the end of their stay, to "replace all doors when you leave a house."[5] Since doors in Chinese peasant homes often were detached and laid flat for use as beds at night, this last rule actually was an order for Red Army soldiers to make their beds.

Of course, the army's main job was not to be nice, but to fight and defeat the GMD enemy. Mao was a confirmed believer in the use of violence to make a

5. Quoted in Edgar Snow, *Red Star Over China* (New York: Random House, 1938), pp. 157–158.

revolution. As he put it in his most famous statement on the subject:

> A revolution is not the same as inviting people to dinner, or writing an essay, or painting a picture, or doing fancy needlework; it cannot be anything so refined and gentle, or so mild, kind, courteous, restrained, and magnanimous. A revolution is an uprising, an act of violence whereby one class overthrows another.[6]

Nor did Mao limit his use of violence to the GMD. He also wielded it ruthlessly against his opponents in the party, both before the party came to power and well after it controlled China.

A third principle of Mao's thinking was the idea that human will could overcome virtually any obstacle. This principle, like Mao's views on the peasantry, violated traditional Marxism, which stressed that socialism could be achieved only by modern industrial societies. But Mao believed that a technologically backward society could achieve miracles if its people were inspired by the correct ideas. This required that the party use education and propaganda, and force if necessary, to control how people thought. During the early 1930s, Mao's ideas about human will and correct thinking usually remained in the background as the party struggled to survive. But these ideas became more important as Mao's stature and the party's power grew. In the 1950s and 1960s, once the party had van-

6. Mao Tse-tung, *Selected Works*, vol. 1, 1926–1936 (New York, International Publishers, 1954), p. 27.

quished its enemies, Mao's ideas became central to disputes over policy that nearly tore the party apart.

However, no amount of force or human will Mao could muster could save the organization he built during the early 1930s. The Chinese Soviet Republic proclaimed in 1931 was under continual GMD attack. In 1934, overwhelmed by Chiang's German-aided troops, Mao and his followers were forced to abandon their base in Jiangxi and run for their lives. That flight, with GMD forces in hot pursuit, lasted over a year and is known as the "Long March." Fighting almost every day, the Red Army traveled 6,000 miles (9,650 kilometers), crossing twelve provinces, eighteen mountain ranges, and twenty-four rivers. In the middle of it all, the CCP paused for a conference at which it chose Mao as its new leader. In October 1935, Mao's forces arrived in Shanxi Province in northern China. But the joy of escaping from the enemy's clutches was muted by the agony of defeat: Of the 100,000 people who began the Long March, only 10 percent finished.

Yet to the CCP the Long March was like Valley Forge to George Washington's troops. The key point was that the CCP had endured and survived. Many of the Long March commanders, including Lin Biao, Liu Shaoqi, and Deng Xiaoping, were to become the party's top leaders for decades. In addition, the survivors came away with a new sense of mission and a confidence in Mao and his ability to lead the party. But as Mao pointed out, the party had been dealt another devastating blow. It had been driven from its base in Jiangxi and suffered heavy losses during the Long March. It had to rebuild once again. In 1936, after they moved their headquarters to the town of Yan'an, that is exactly what Mao and the party leadership began to do.

Mao Zedong in Yan'an in 1937.

Japan, World War II, and the Communist Victory

While the Nationalists and Communists were fighting each other, millions of Chinese looked fearfully northward to the Japanese in Manchuria. The Japanese army was poised to attack China in force, and the Chinese people wanted their politicians to unite against the foreign aggressor who already controlled Manchuria. That pressure produced a partnership known as the Second United Front between the CCP and the GMD. However, it wasn't achieved until Chiang was kidnapped in December 1936 by one of his own generals and was forced to agree to the new partnership as the condition of his release. In reality, the Second United Front was a forced marriage between two mutually hostile partners who fought each other as often as they fought the Japanese. Each leader used it for his own purposes: Chiang to build his prestige as China's leader, and Mao to build the CCP's strength while undermining the GMD.

The Japanese launched their full-scale invasion of China in July 1937. They struck with the same savagery and mercilessness they had displayed elsewhere in Asia, from Korea to Malaya to the Philippines. In China the Japanese were guilty of indiscriminate bombing, the ruthless slaughter of civilians, the use of poisonous gases, and rampant rape and torture. By the time the Japanese were finally defeated in 1945, between 15 and 20 million Chinese were dead. The symbol of Japanese aggression in China was the infamous 1937 "rape of Nanjing," a rampage of killing, rape, and looting that left over 150,000 civilians dead, thousands of women ravaged, and Chiang's former capital city in ruins.

The war with Japan, which after 1939 became part of World War II in the Pacific, dealt a devastating blow to the Guomindang. Chiang's forces were no match for the modern Japanese war machine, in part because of the corruption and mismanagement that riddled the GMD. After brave resistance by Chinese troops in cities like Nanjing, Chiang's strategy became to "trade space for time." He decided to retreat into China's vast interior and wait for outside help.

That help did come in the form of military aid from the United States, especially after Japan bombed Pearl Harbor and brought about America's entrance into World War II in December 1941. However, American military advisers sent to help China justifiably complained that Chiang's regime was corrupt and was wasting the help it was receiving. Nevertheless, Chiang's strategy did help, in the short run, to save the GMD regime by allowing him to husband his resources for what he considered his most important battle: the postwar showdown with the Communists. In Chiang's opinion, the Japanese, despite their military power, were a "disease of the skin," but the Communists, with their following among the Chinese people, were a "disease of the heart."

However, the loss of China's coastal region and its major cities left the GMD without its main pillars of financial and social support. Chiang's retreat also left hundreds of millions of Chinese without leadership against the invaders. And in the areas Chiang controlled, he taxed the people to the bone to make up for revenue losses from the Japanese-occupied areas and to support his increasingly corrupt regime. Foreign observers described what they saw in the areas Chiang still controlled:

> The peasants . . . were dying. They were lying on the roads, in the mountains, by the railway stations, in the mud huts, in the fields. And as they died, the government continued to wring from them the last possible ounce of tax. . . . The government in county after county was demanding more actual poundage of grain than [a farmer] had raised on his acres. No excuses were allowed; peasants who were eating elm bark and dried leaves had to haul their last sack of grain to the tax collector's office. . . . Peasants who could not pay were forced to the wall; they sold their cattle, their furniture, and even their land to buy grain to meet the tax quotas.[7]

While Chiang and the GMD left their people to fend for themselves, the Chinese Communist party under the skilled and ruthless leadership of Mao Zedong stepped daringly into the breach. The Japanese invasion, as it ripped gaping wounds into the body of China and plunged a sword into the GMD, also broke the iron grip the GMD had on the CCP's throat. With the GMD driven from huge parts of China, CCP agents were able to move in and organize resistance against the Japanese. The Communists used their organizing skills and expertise in guerrilla warfare to win peasant support and control of large sections of the Chinese countryside. As

---

7. Theodore White and Annalee Jacoby, *Thunder Out of China* (New York: William Sloan Associates, 1946), pp. 174–175.

they did so, the CCP won the respect not only of the peasantry and workers, their traditional constituencies, but of other classes of Chinese as well. The CCP, not the GMD, increasingly represented resistance and hence Chinese nationalism as the Chinese people did desperate battle with Japan.

The Communists also used the Second United Front to their advantage. It provided an opportunity for Communist cadres to infiltrate the GMD army and governmental administration. It also gave the CCP respectability, since it was officially in partnership with the ruling party. To enhance that image, the CCP usually followed moderate policies in the areas it controlled. For example, instead of seizing land and giving it to the peasants, the CCP usually just enforced GMD laws that put limits on rents, laws the GMD itself did not enforce. These and similar practices, which reached out beyond peasants and workers to small businessmen and even some capitalists, broadened the CCP's base of support among Chinese of all classes who opposed the Japanese and wanted China to have effective government.

The most effective methods for building the CCP's strength were policies that together came to be called the "Yan'an Way" after the town where the party was headquartered. The Yan'an Way built strong ties between the CCP and its main constituency, the peasantry. It also created extraordinary spirit among the party cadres. During the Yan'an years, Red Army troops, intellectuals, and government officials could be found growing crops along with the peasants or working in makeshift factories located in caves. According to a doctrine known as the "mass line," party cadres in a village did not simply give orders, but were expected to learn about the peasants' problems and to share the hardships of their lives. And when it came time to act—for example, against an oppressive landlord—it was essential that the peasants themselves take action. In other words, while the CCP had to provide leadership, it could not make the revolution *for* the peasants. It had to mobilize them so that they participated directly in overturning the old order. Only if the people themselves were directly involved, Mao insisted, could the revolution succeed. Of course, when persuasion failed, Mao and the CCP leadership did not hesitate to use force, either against peasants or dissident party members.

Other Yan'an Way policies included using education and literacy campaigns to spread party propaganda. Mao also developed a harsh but effective method of indoctrinating CCP cadres called *zhengfeng*. It relied on submitting the cadres to months of intense group pressure, including long, grinding, and often brutal criticism sessions, to rid them of any ideas that violated the party's version of the truth. While all this was going on, Mao was raised above all other party leaders and increasingly was taking on the stature of a Communist prophet or living saint. Cadres were taught to accept without question his version of the truth. In 1943 he was made chairman of the party, a post created especially for him. When the party adopted a new constitution, the document included a section on the "Thought of Mao Zedong." In effect, just as Russia had produced its versions of Marxism called Leninism and Stalinism, a new variant of Marxism called "Maoism" was taking shape in China.

The new policies developed in Yan'an were enormously successful. When World War II ended in 1945,

Mao on the march with soldiers during the civil
war that broke out following World War II.

the CCP was in a powerful position. In 1937, it was a battered force of 40,000 members in command of an army of 80,000 and in control of about 1.5 million poverty-stricken peasants. Eight years later, the 1.2-million-member CCP fielded an army of 900,000 and controlled a large part of China with a population of 90 million people. In 1946, a civil war began—the final test of strength between the CCP and GMD. Although the GMD, supported by extensive aid from the United States, won some initial victories, the tide soon turned. The GMD was crumbling from within, while the CCP had built a solid and wide base of support. By 1949, the civil war was over. In March, Mao Zedong rode victoriously into Beijing in a captured American jeep and on October 1, 1949, triumphantly proclaimed the establishment of the People's Republic of China (PRC). Once again, China stood uncertainly between two worlds: the dead world of the capitalist Chinese Republic and the yet to be born Communist world of the People's Republic of China. Standing like a mountain before the Chinese Communist party was the immense task of giving birth to that new world and making it a better one for China's half a billion people.

SOCIALIST CHINA

Shortly before Mao Zedong officially proclaimed the establishment of the People's Republic of China in China's newly designated capital of Beijing, he proudly told the Chinese people and the world:

> Our work will go down in the history of mankind, demonstrating that the Chinese people, comprising one quarter of humanity, have now stood up. . . . Ours will no longer be a nation subject to insult and humiliation. We have stood up.[1]

Mao was right: The Communist victory meant that, along with the GMD, the foreign powers that had taken advantage of China for one hundred years had been

1. *Selected Works of Mao Tse-tung*, vol. 5 (Beijing: Foreign Languages Press, 1977), pp. 16–17.

banished from the country. But if China, as Mao put it, had stood up, it also was still suffering. With the exception of a ten-month break between September 1945 and July 1946, China had been at war since 1937. The economy was close to collapse and terrible hardship was widespread. Industrial production was barely half that of the prewar years, and food production was 25 percent below previous years. War and civil war had created millions of refugees. The Communist party, despite years of experience governing rural areas, knew very little about how to manage the large and complex cities that had just fallen into its hands. Virtually everything needed to build a modern nation, from skilled workers to essential materials, was in short supply. Meanwhile, the Guomindang under Chiang, which had fled to the island of Taiwan 110 miles (177 kilometers) off the coast, continued air and naval raids against the mainland.

Recovery and Consolidation

During the party's long struggle for power, Mao had often demonstrated his ability to control his revolutionary idealism when restraint and moderation were necessary to solve urgent problems. In the years immediately after 1949, he did so again. As he told his followers, before they did anything, "We should get ourselves better organized."[2]

One aspect of getting better organized was to complete the conquest of the outlying areas of China

2. Quoted in Stephen Uhalley, Jr., A *History of the Chinese Communist Party* (Stanford, Calif.: Hoover Institution Press, 1988), p. 83

not yet under Communist control. Aside from Taiwan, four major territories, three of which were largely populated by minority nationalities, were involved: Inner Mongolia, an arid territory north of the Great Wall; Xinjiang, a largely Turkic/Islamic area northwest of China proper; Tibet, the huge plateau and mountain region whose people had a long history of independence under the rule of the Dalai Lama, their Buddhist spiritual leader; and Hainan Island, southeast of Guangzhou near Vietnam. By the end of 1950, most of these areas had been brought under Beijing's control, although not without resistance. Opposition was especially strong in Tibet, which was invaded by Communist forces in October 1950. Tibetans protested to an unlistening world against what the CCP called the "liberation" of their country:

> Liberation from whom and from what? Ours is a happy country with a solvent government.[3]

Far more important than control of the outlying areas was control of the countryside in China proper. The Communist military victory did not change the system of landlord and clan relationships that left most Chinese peasants living in poverty and deep in debt on tiny scraps of land. Determined to break this power structure once and for all, in 1950 the CCP announced a land-reform law that took the land from the landlords and distributed it among the peasantry. Teams of party cadres were sent to the villages to carry out the new

3. Quoted in Jonathan Spence, *The Search for Modern China* (New York: Norton, 1990), p. 525.

law. Following the ideas of the mass line, they were expected to get the peasants themselves to denounce their landlords during "struggle meetings." Peasants were to "speak bitterness" and unmask the tyrants of the old regime. But the party cadres often ran into serious problems, in part because the enormous task of reaching all the villages outstripped the number of qualified personnel. Many of those sent to the villages were untrained and inexperienced in working with peasants. Furthermore, the poor peasants who were expected to help the party workers often did not, either because they were not hostile to their landlords (sometimes landlord and tenant belonged to the same clan) or because they feared them. More than twenty centuries of landlord rule, enforced by brutal punishment of those who dared to defy the authorities, had instilled a paralysis among the peasantry that was passed on from generation to generation. In one village, an American reporter recorded experiences that were typical of what went on all over China:

> The first stop of the overturning movement is to "struggle" against landlords and divide the land. They [the cadres] announced that every village had the right to elect its own officials and that land rents and rates of interest should be reduced. The people listened half-heartedly, kept their mouths tightly shut and went home without speaking further to the cadres.

Finally, after a peasant who had dared to talk to the CCP cadres was found murdered, the cadres were able to use that crime to get some peasants to speak out publicly. Among them was the murdered man's wife. A "struggle meeting" in which peasants took turns at "speaking bitterness" followed, then another. The landlord's spell over the village was broken, and he paid a heavy price upon being judged by a vengeful "people's court":

> A slight shiver of apprehension went through the audience. They could not believe their enemy was helpless before them.
>
> The poorest peasant stepped forward.
>
> "Now the time has come for our revenge!" he announced in a trembling voice. "In what way shall we take revenge on this sinful landlord? We shall kill him."
>
> He turned round and slapped Wang [the landlord] on the face. A low animal moan broke from the crowd and it leaped into action. The landlord gave one chilling shriek and then bowed his head in resignation. The crowd was on him like beasts. . . .[4]

By the time the Communist party's campaign was finished in 1952, it had taken the lives of over one million landlords, whose land was then divided up among the peasants. About half of the land in China changed hands, with the poorest peasants gaining the most. However, the land-reform program did not create a socialist agricultural system, which to the CCP meant large collective farms worked by dozens or even hundreds of families. Instead, millions of individual peasant farmers owned their land, and some peasants had

4. Jack Belden, *China Shakes the World* (New York: Monthly Review Press, 1970), pp. 242–253.

more land and were more prosperous than others. But by destroying the power of the landlords, the CCP shattered a power structure that had existed for centuries and cleared the way for further changes. As for the violence that destroyed the landlord class, that did not bother Mao and other party leaders. The CCP chairman explained his cold and calculated reasoning:

> Whom have we executed? What sort of people? Elements for whom the masses had great hatred. If we did not kill some tyrants, or if we were too lenient with them, the masses would not agree.[5]

The land reform proved to be one step in a successful economic recovery. Land reform helped China to produce three consecutive desperately needed good harvests, beginning in 1950. Another important step was in getting most of China's railroads back into service as early as 1950. In the cities, the government took over many industries, including most railways and heavy industries like coal and steel. But there were significant exceptions. Choosing practical necessity over Communist idealism, the CCP left some businesses in private hands, including several fairly large factories. These privately held businesses contributed significantly to the country's economic recovery. By 1952, many industries had topped their best pre-1949 production records.

Along with land reform, the marriage-reform law was the most drastic of the CCP's early reforms and affected the most people. The law was an attempt to

---

5. Quoted in Harrison E. Salisbury, *China: 100 Years of Revolution* (New York: Holt, Rinehart and Winston, 1983), p. 199.

leap from the state of affairs reflected in the old Chinese saying that "a wife married is like a pony bought; I'll ride her and whip her as I like" to Mao's remark that "women hold up half the sky." The law forbade arranged or forced marriages and made wives equal to their husbands in terms of property ownership and the right to seek divorce. It also protected children, making it illegal to sell or kill them, a practice that most often victimized unwanted daughters. Other reforms included a massive and highly successful campaign against opium addiction, which included rehabilitation of addicts and, significantly, the rounding up and quick execution of opium sellers. And a campaign against prostitution was also very successful. Like the land-reform and anti-opium campaigns, it relied heavily on the tools of the Communist police state the CCP was building. These included party-controlled neighborhood committees that spied on everyone and meted out harsh penalties with little regard for formal judicial procedures that might have allowed those accused to defend themselves.

In fact, even before the CCP was able to begin building a socialist society, it was establishing what is known as a totalitarian state. Totalitarianism is a twentieth-century phenomenon in which the state, making use of modern technology, controls almost every aspect of human life. All institutions, from the army and police to trade unions, youth organizations, schools, news organizations, and even sports clubs, are controlled by the state. Citizens have no constitutional protection against the state and its police. A single party, in China's case the CCP, controls the state. It is the only party allowed to exist, and its version of the truth is the only point of view that can be expressed. In some totalitarian states, such as Nazi Germany, the bulk of the economy remained in private hands. In socialist totalitarian states, such as the Soviet Union and the People's Republic of China, the state eventually took control of the economy.

By the early 1950s, the PRC was a fully formed totalitarian state. In the late 1950s and again in the mid-1960s, totalitarian pressures on the Chinese people would be intensified, and millions of people would suffer terribly as a result.

Foreign Affairs

Prior to 1949, the CCP under Mao was not on particularly good terms with the Soviet Union under Stalin. Mao had consistently ignored Stalin's advice and had led the CCP on an independent course by basing the Chinese revolution on the peasantry. Stalin mistrusted Communists who dared to show any independence, and in fact usually killed those he could get his hands on. He showed his distaste for Mao and the CCP by giving them very little help and by insulting them as well. Mao and his followers in the CCP, said Stalin, were "radish" Communists, red on the outside but white on the inside. As for the Chinese revolution itself, Stalin considered it a "fake."

Despite their mutual dislike, the Soviet and Chinese Communists nonetheless needed each other. Stalin needed any ally he could find in his Cold War struggle with the United States, while Mao desperately needed economic help to rebuild his battered country. With the Soviet Union and the United States locked in their Cold War conflict, the PRC considered it logical to "lean to one side," that side being the Soviet side in the Cold War. In December 1949, Mao therefore journeyed to Moscow to meet with Stalin. Instead of being welcomed as the comrade and hero he considered himself to be, however, Mao was treated coldly and was ignored by the Soviet press. After long and difficult negotiations, a thirty-year Sino-Soviet Treaty of Friendship, Alliance, and Mutual Assistance was signed. The treaty disappointed the Chinese. It provided them with $60 million worth of loans per year for five years, not the grants they had expected. This small package was less than half the value of the industrial equipment the Soviets took home from Manchuria after they liberated the region from the Japanese in 1945. The Soviets also retained privileges in Manchuria and other parts of northern China that the old Russian Empire had secured from the Manchu dynasty in the nineteenth century. Although much was made of the new alliance between the world's Communist giants, especially in the West, in fact it really only papered over deep differences between the Russians and the Chinese. Within a decade, the paper the treaty was written on had worn thin enough for any keen observer to see through.

The year 1950, which began for China with a treaty of friendship with the Soviet Union, ended in a bloody war with the United States. In June, the Communist North Korean government had sent its Soviet-equipped army across the 38th parallel, its border with non-Communist South Korea. Deeply concerned about further Communist expansion in Asia, the United States persuaded the United Nations Security Council to condemn the invasion and to authorize its members to send troops to defend South Korea. Most of the foreign troops sent to South Korea were Americans, although they officially fought under the banner of the United Nations. By September, UN forces had

U.S. *troops fire on enemy positions during the Korean War.*

turned the tide in Korea, crossed the 38th parallel, and were moving quickly northward toward the North Korean–Chinese border. The Chinese were determined to prevent the destruction of the North Korean regime. They also did not want the American army to reach the Chinese-Korean border, which was close to important industrial sites in Manchuria. The CCP waited until November, and then ordered hundreds of thousands of troops into Korea. The Chinese surprised the badly outnumbered Americans and once again drove them south of the 38th parallel.

The Korean War became a grinding hill-by-hill struggle. The United States used its superior firepower to return to the approximate line of the 38th parallel. But the fighting dragged on until 1953 and cost the Chinese dearly. They suffered about 1 million casualties, including 300,000 dead, among them Mao Zedong's son. The war bled China's already anemic economy. It robbed China of vital materials and skilled workers, interrupted the education of hundreds of thousands of students who were drafted into the army, and drained the country of many of its doctors, needed to care for the wounded. The United States' losses amounted to over 54,000 dead, and Korea's suffering was catastrophic. At least 2 million Koreans died, and their country was left divided and in ruins.

Finally, the Korean War brought the United States to the aid of Chiang Kai-shek and the Nationalists on Taiwan. Prior to the outbreak of the war the United States appeared to accept that the Communists would soon invade and conquer Taiwan. Immediately after the North Korean invasion, the United States sent naval forces into the strait between Taiwan and the mainland to protect the vulnerable Nationalist regime.

Military support was followed by additional United States aid, which guaranteed the survival of the Nationalists and frustrated and infuriated the Communists.

On the diplomatic front, the United States refused to recognize the CCP regime as the legitimate government of China, continuing to recognize the Nationalists on Taiwan instead. It also prevented the PRC's admission to the UN, while leaving the Nationalists with China's seat in both the General Assembly and the Security Council. Although it lasted only three years, the Korean War thus prevented the total unification of China under Communist rule and froze United States–Chinese relations in a state of bitter hostility for a generation.

Hysteria and Repression

The Korean War also turned the hostility in China against real or imagined enemies of the new order into hysteria, and contributed to new and bloody waves of repression that swept through the country during the early 1950s. These began with campaigns directly related to the Korean War, such as the Resist America and Aid-Korea campaigns. In February 1951 the Suppression of Counterrevolutionaries campaign began, which claimed hundreds of thousands of lives. An American historian has described how the campaign took a far greater toll than even those numbers suggest:

> The public was encouraged to participate in the witch hunt. Youngsters who denounced

their own parents were praised. Party members who tried to protect targeted family members were themselves punished. . . . The word quickly spread that many people were being taken arbitrarily and then subjected to frightening mass trials before being executed. Many others were sentenced to forced labor or imprisonment.[6]

The offensive against counterrevolutionaries was succeeded by two other campaigns: the "Three Anti-Movement" and the "Five Anti-Movement." The former—directed against corruption, waste, and bureaucracy—was aimed at party officials and lasted from September 1951 until April 1952. The latter—against bribery, tax evasion, fraud, the stealing of government property, and the stealing of state economic information—had China's remaining private businessmen as its primary target. Everything from mass demonstrations to booming kettledrums was used to whip up hatred against people the government denounced as "tigers." By the end of the campaign, only a broken remnant was left of China's business community, which was fated to disappear entirely within the next few years.

By 1953, reform and repression had solidified Communist power in China. The cost in "local despots," "tigers," "counterrevolutionaries," "bandits," "secret agents," and similar enemies of the new order probably reached a total of five million dead and possibly even more. To the leadership of the CCP, this was a small price to pay for what it considered to be

6. Uhalley, p. 101.

progress. The time had come to move on, from securing power in China to turning China into a socialist society.

Building Socialism: The First
Five-Year Plan and Collectivization

In Marxist China, as in the Marxist Soviet Union, building socialism meant that the state would run the entire economy and would use all available resources to build modern industry. Without modern industry, Marxist ideology insisted, no society could achieve the high standard of living required to fulfill Marx's ideal of "from each according to his ability, to each according to his needs."

Mao might not have admired Stalin and many Soviet methods, but the fact was that in 1949 the Soviet Union under Stalin's dictatorship provided the only Marxist model for rapid economic development and the building of socialism. Under the Soviet model, all important decisions were made by central planners, who in turn took their orders from the Communist party leadership. The Soviet Union had taken a two-pronged approach to industrialization, using a series of five-year plans beginning in the late 1920s. First, most Soviet investments went into basic heavy industries, such as steel, coal, and industrial machinery, that were essential to building military might. All other sectors of the Soviet economy, such as consumer goods and agriculture, were starved to feed heavy industry. Second, all Soviet peasants lost their private farms and were put to work on state-controlled collective farms, which were far larger and were supposed to make use of modern machinery and production techniques.

In building industry, the CCP, relying heavily on Soviet advisers, followed the Soviet model quite closely when it initiated its first five-year plan in 1953. Almost 60 percent of all investment went to heavy industry. Of 700 major industrial projects, the Soviet Union supplied aid in the form of thousands of engineers, blueprints, and other technological assistance on 156 key projects. However, unlike the aid the United States gave its allies, Soviet aid to China continued to be loans that had to be repaid as early as the mid-1950s. During the 1950s, there were well over 10,000 Soviet experts working in China, while more than 80,000 Chinese went to study in the Soviet Union. The results of the industrialization drive were impressive. When the first five-year plan ended in 1957, total industrial production had more than doubled, while key heavy industries had done even better. For example, coal production doubled, steel production more than tripled, and the generation of electric power also almost tripled. The production of locomotives rose by eight times, and a truck-building industry was built from the ground up.

The other half of the industrial equation was agriculture, which was expected to support the industrialization effort with increased production of both food and industrial crops such as cotton. New investments were not going to do the job, since the first five-year plan allotted only 7.6 percent of all investment to agriculture, an area in which 90 percent of all Chinese worked. The key was to reorganize agriculture. Small private plots worked by hand would be replaced by large collective farms using masses of labor and, when available, modern machinery. However, unlike in industry, the CCP had years of experience in working with peasants, beginning in the 1920s during the First United Front and continuing through the years in Jiangxi and Yan'an. In addition, the CCP knew the terrible history of Soviet collectivization. Against intense opposition and in just a few years, the Soviets had rammed collectivization down the throats of the peasantry. The result was catastrophic. Peasants who resisted collectivization were shot, and at least five million died in a famine the government itself caused when it seized all the peasants' grain. Millions more, including most of the wealthier and most capable peasants, were forbidden to join the collectives and were instead sent to be worked to death in labor camps or were deported to remote areas of the country. Property was destroyed, millions of farm animals were lost, and production dropped rather than increased.

Because the Soviet example was so disastrous, the CCP developed its own methods of collectivization. Its most important innovation was to carry out the process in three stages. Collectivization began in 1953 with what were called "mutual aid teams" in which a few families worked together on specific projects while retaining their own land. The second stage was the "lower Agricultural Producers' Cooperatives" (APCs) in which twenty to forty families combined their land and resources. However, they were paid in part for how much land they brought to the cooperative, a policy that maintained differences based on property. The next stage, the "higher APCs," were full collective farms. Several hundred families worked and lived together on farms where all land and tools belonged to the collective as a whole.

A young boy helps out on a large communal farm. By the late 1950s most Chinese peasants lived on such farms.

Although the violence of the Soviet experience was avoided, collectivization yielded disappointing results. Production barely increased. Not only was the rate of increase far lower than the 1950–1953 period *before* collectivization, but it was less than the growth of the population, and the output of some crops important to industry, such as cotton, actually dropped. In addition, many peasants, notably the more successful ones, resisted collectivization, especially once it got beyond the stage of mutual-aid teams. Furthermore, in many areas there was not enough machinery to justify these larger farms. Faced with these problems, many party leaders urged that collectivization be slowed down to avoid disrupting the countryside. They argued that a slower pace would in the end produce more-productive collective farms. Among them were Zhou Enlai, the country's premier, Chen Yun, the party's leading economist, and Liu Shaoqi, an able veteran of many battles who ranked just below Mao in the party hierarchy. One of the CCP's top agricultural experts spoke for these leaders when he said:

> We [lack] the necessary conditions [for collectivization]. . . . Moreover, the Chinese peasants' conception of private ownership is relatively deep, while our task is heavy and we have not enough cadres.[7]

Mao strongly disagreed. Whereas in the 1940s and early 1950s the party chairman had been willing to adjust policies in order to cope with practical problems, Mao was beginning to change. He told the party:

7. Quoted in Parris Chang, *Policy and Power in China* (University Park: Pennsylvania State University Press, 1975), p. 10.

But some of our comrades are tottering along like a woman with bound feet and constantly complaining, "You are going too fast." Excessive criticism, inappropriate complaints, endless anxiety, and the erection of countless taboos—they believe this is the proper way to guide the socialist mass movement in the rural areas.

No, this is not the right way; it is the wrong way.[8]

The disagreement between Mao and his opponents led to heated disputes and swings in party policy between 1954 and 1956. Eventually each side came away with something. By 1957, most peasants were living on higher Agricultural Producers' Cooperatives. But against Mao's wishes, peasants were allowed to keep tiny private plots they could work in their spare time, where they could raise vegetables or farm animals such as pigs and chickens. Much to Mao's dismay, the peasants showed far more interest in their private plots than in working the fields of the collectives. In 1956, for example, they earned 20 to 30 percent of their income from private plots that were only 5 percent of China's agricultural land.

Disputes, Criticism, and Repression

By the fall of 1956, divisions were beginning to appear among the men at the top of the CCP. Prior to that, they

8. Harold C. Hinton, ed., *The People's Republic of China, 1949–1979: A Documentary Survey*, vol. 1 1949–1957 (Wilmington, Del.: Scholarly Resources, 1980), p. 51.

China's leaders posed for this picture in 1963. Mao is at the center, with Deng Xiaoping on his right and Peng Zhen on his left. Zhou Enlai is third from Mao's left.

had worked together to win power, consolidate their control over China, stand up to the mighty United States, and begin building socialism. At the party's Eighth Congress in September, the delegates adopted a new constitution that dropped references to the "Thought of Mao Zedong." Mao's power as party chairman was limited when the Congress set up a powerful post, general secretary. Deng Xiaoping, a respected Long March veteran who was appointed to the post, clearly had Mao in mind when he warned against what he called "deification of the individual." Liu Shaoqi, whose sharp mind was matched by a sharp tongue, was even more to the point. He reminded the party:

> . . . there is no such thing as a perfect leader, either in the past or the present, either in China or elsewhere. If there is one, he is only pretending, like a pig inserting scallions into his nose in a effort to look like an elephant.[9]

The disputes among the party's top leaders led to an unusual episode known as the Hundred Flowers Campaign, in which Mao and the party actually asked the country's intellectuals to criticize the party's performance. Mao had several motives for pushing the campaign. He seems to have believed that various "thought reform" campaigns directed against intellectuals during the early and mid-1950s had won them over to the Communist cause. He expected that their criticism would be mild, "a gentle wind and fine rain," as he described it, and that the opportunity to speak openly would increase their support for the Communist order. Mao thought this criticism would improve the conduct of the party bureaucracy, which he feared sometimes treated the people in a high-handed manner. At least as important, the chairman, without any evidence, assumed that the country's intellectuals agreed with him and that their remarks would help him against his opponents among the party leadership.

9. Quoted in Witold Rodzinsky, *The People's Republic of China: A Concise Political History* (New York: The Free Press, 1988), p. 49.

Finally, Mao had been shaken by the 1956 anti-Communist revolt in Hungary, one of the Soviet-dominated states in Eastern Europe. The lesson of that revolt, he thought, was that the party had to listen more to the population at large to avoid the tensions that had exploded into revolt in Hungary.

In April 1957, under the slogan "Let a hundred flowers bloom, let a hundred schools of thought contend," intellectuals were asked to speak their minds. For a while they hesitated; the memories of earlier Communist repression were still fresh in their minds. More encouragement to speak out eventually brought results, but what took place was more like a cloudburst than a fine rain. Party members were denounced for enjoying privileges that made them "a race apart." Mao's earlier mass campaigns were labeled "a serious violation of human rights" and "tyranny." A teacher denied that peasants wanted to join the collectives. "As a matter of fact," he wrote, "the majority of them are forced to join. A professor called the Communist administrators at his university "feudal princes and stinking charlatans."[10]

Mao and the party were shocked and responded with a vengeance. Those who had dared to speak openly, including party members and ordinary workers, were denounced as "rightists." They became the victims of the "anti-rightist" campaign of 1957–1958. Over 500,000 intellectuals, including many of China's most brilliant scientists, found their careers ruined. The stigma of being a "rightist" was often passed down to their children. Like the children of former landlords, capitalists, and other "bad classes," boys and girls with

10. Quoted in Spence, p. 570.

"rightist" parents found themselves denounced at school and denied opportunities for advancement.

Many intellectuals ended up in labor camps or were exiled to remote villages in the countryside. There they lived for years in grinding poverty and, even worse, in isolation from the world of ideas that was the basis of their lives. One boy later described what happened to his mother, who had made a few minor criticisms only after being strongly encouraged to do so by her superiors:

> There were all types of people [in the camp] . . . but friendships were impossible because the best strategy . . . was to report on others. Thus everyone was always watching everyone else, and a grain of rice dropped on the floor could mean an afternoon of criticism for disrespecting the labors of the peasants. Everything was fair game, even what people said in their sleep.
>
> The second essential strategy was to write constant Thought Reports about oneself. Few of the people in the camp thought they were Rightists, but the only thing to do was to confess one's crimes . . . and invent things to repent. . . .
>
> The last important route to freedom was hard work. One had to deliberately add to one's misery in small ways, like going without a hat under the hot summer sun or continuing to work in the rain after everyone else had quit. . . . Sometimes they were taken in trucks to special laboring areas to break and carry stones. . . . Still, bear it she did . . . and

after three long years, when she could carry more than a hundred pounds of rocks on her back with ease, a bored-looking official . . . told her she was no longer a Rightist. She could go home.[11]

Mao tried to make the best of an embarrassing situation. He insisted that his plan all along had been to draw out from their hiding places the "demons and devils, ghosts, and monsters" who opposed the revolution, and then to "wipe them out."[12] In any event, the party leadership, despite some differences of opinion, had survived the self-inflicted Hundred Flowers and Anti-Rightist episodes largely intact. That would not be the case in the next crisis they would create. the catastrophic Great Leap Forward.

11. Liang Heng and Judith Shapiro, *Son of the Revolution* (New York: Vintage Books, 1984), pp. 12–13.

12. Quoted in Dick Wilson, *The People's Emperor, Mao: A Biography of Mao Tse-tung* (New York: Lee Publishers Group), p. 347.

THE GREAT
LEAP FORWARD

By 1957 the Chinese Communist party had much to show for its efforts since winning control of China in 1949. It was firmly entrenched in power. Chiang Kai-shek and the Nationalists on Taiwan were a frustrating, sometimes infuriating nuisance, but they were not a threat to Communist rule on the mainland. The CCP had destroyed the power of the landed gentry by 1952 and had then successfully collectivized over 500 million peasants during the first five-year plan. Industrial growth under state control during that plan had been impressive, although the job of making China a modern industrial power had in reality only just begun. Sweeping social reforms such as the 1950 Marriage Law and campaigns against drug use and prostitution had also been highly successful. Foreign powers had been driven from China, and its People's Liberation Army had stood up to the United States military in Korea for almost three years. Meanwhile, China had won a respected place in the international arena, especially in the eyes of the growing number of newly independent nations of Asia and Africa. These countries admired China for standing up to the former colonial powers and saw the PRC as an exciting new model of how to begin the long ascent out of poverty and backwardness.

But like a deep gnawing ache an athlete can ignore in the heat of competition but can barely endure once the cheering stops, concern over how China's revolution was taking shape nagged at Chairman Mao. Some of that concern had to do with unsatisfactory numbers. While the first five-year plan had produced a high rate of industrial growth, it had failed to significantly increase agricultural production. This failure threatened China's future economic growth. Not only would it leave China without resources to pay for the aid it was receiving from the Soviet Union, but the CCP would soon be unable to feed its huge population. China's first systematic census in 1953 had shown that instead of an expected 450 million people, its population stood at 580 million. And that figure was growing by 2 percent per year, double the 1 percent rate at which grain production rose in 1957.

But for Mao and his supporters, these numbers, while important, were less worrisome than the methods China was using to build socialism. The crux of the issue rested on one of Mao's bedrock beliefs: the only way to build socialism was by strictly socialist methods. Any compromise with socialist methods— and Mao from the beginning set himself up as the sole judge of what made up those methods—would sabotage the effort to reach socialism. That was why, during the mid-1950s, Mao opposed allowing peasants to keep small private plots during collectivization. He feared that the peasants would use those plots to buy and sell in the old capitalist style, and that those activities would lure them away from socialism.

Mao also worried about the Soviet-style central-planning methods that China followed during the first five-year plan. Under the Soviet system, all decisions were made by central planners. The people did as they were told. This violated Mao's principle of the "mass line" that had been so successful in Yan'an, under which the party leadership was to work hand in hand with the people to solve problems. Soviet central planning had another fault: Its emphasis on building modern industry left few resources for agriculture and the countryside. Mao outlined some of what was wrong with this as early as 1956. Not only did what he considered the overemphasis on heavy industry hurt the peasantry—in other words, most of the people—but it was in the end self-defeating precisely in terms of heavy industry:

> The . . . development of heavy industry without regard for people's lives . . . brings discontent in its wake . . . and heavy industry cannot progress. This way, in the long run heavy industry develops more slowly and not as well.[1]

Mao believed that the CCP was having these difficulties because it was relying on foreign models rather than on its own experience. In particular, Mao did not like the idea of copying the Soviet Union, whose methods, advice, and strategy he had found lacking since the 1920s. Not only in economics, Mao said, but

1. Quoted in Jean Chexneaux, *China: The People's Republic, 1949–1976* (New York: Pantheon Books, 1979), p. 84.

in everything from education to health matters the Chinese had sold themselves short and had relied too much on the Soviet Union. In early 1958, Mao maintained that this blind subservience had gone so far that it literally ruined his diet:

> We did not even study our own experience in education in the Liberated Areas [territory under CCP control before 1949]. The same applied to our public health work, with the result that I couldn't have eggs or chicken soup for three years because an article appeared in the Soviet Union which said that one shouldn't eat them. Later they said one should eat them. It didn't matter whether the article was correct or not, the Chinese listened all the time and respectfully obeyed. In short, the Soviet Union was tops.[2]

The Soviet Union was held in such awe, Mao added, that even physical accuracy was sacrificed. He complained that although he was considerably taller than Joseph Stalin, when Chinese artists painted Mao and Stalin together, "they always made me a bit shorter." The time had come for this fawning and imitation to stop:

> We lacked understanding of the whole economic situation and understood still less the economic differences between the Soviet Union and China. So all we could do was follow blindly. Now the situation has

2. "Talks at the Chengtu Conference," March 1958, in Stuart Schram, ed., *Chairman Mao Talks to the People: Talks and Letters, 1956–1971* (New York: Pantheon Books, 1974), p. 98.

changed. Generally speaking, we are capable of undertaking the planning and construction of large enterprises. In another five years we shall be capable of manufacturing the equipment ourselves. We also have some understanding of Soviet and Chinese conditions.[3]

Soviet policies and the dilemmas they caused were not Mao's only difficulties. The chairman was not pleased by what he was hearing from some of his comrades in the CCP leadership. Moderate leaders like Chen Yun, the CCP's leading economist, who was drafting a second five-year plan, and Premier and Foreign Minister Zhou Enlai had their own suggestions for raising food production. They advised giving the peasants material incentives such as higher prices for their crops and more consumer goods to encourage them to work harder and increase production. Chen Yun wanted the PRC to build more factories to produce consumer goods by shifting resources away from basic heavy industries such as steel. But from Mao's point of view, bribing the peasants with consumer goods suffered from the same flaw as allowing them to operate private plots: It was a "capitalist" method that would corrupt them and could therefore never lead to real socialism.

Mao was absolutely convinced that China had to find a better path to socialism, one that he would select. He did not want China to follow another five-year plan according to the Soviet model, nor did he approve of the type of "capitalist" policies Chen Yun was advocating. A debate and struggle over how to

3. Ibid., p. 99.

break out of China's economic rut took place during 1957 and early 1958. At one point the party leadership accepted Mao's radical twelve-year plan for agriculture, but shortly afterward the plan was dropped. When the smoke finally cleared, Mao once again was clearly in charge, helped by the support of Liu Shaoqi and Deng Xiaoping. The result was a new program for economic development based on Mao's increasingly radical ideas. No longer was the party talking about boring plans and endless numbers. Instead, China was about to take a "Great Leap Forward." This great revolutionary act, Mao promised, would enable China to spring out of its pit of backwardness and land ahead of the Soviet Union on the road to complete communism.

The Great Leap Forward

Mao's new strategy reached back to his early theories about the unlimited potential of human will, which he was convinced had been proven correct when the party had overcome many seemingly impossible obstacles during the Yan'an days of the 1930s and 1940s. Mao feared that in the 1950s China was forgetting the lessons of Yan'an and was therefore being held back by a failure of political will. If China could find the will to reorganize itself and adopt the proper policies, it could overcome its economic problems. As Mao put it, rather than let the gloomy economic thinking of party bureaucrats rule China, it was time to "put politics in command," specifically the enlightened politics of the party's chairman. Instead of building socialism "coldly and deliberately," as his opponents wanted, Mao urged the Chinese to go about the job "boldly and joyfully." If that were done, the chairman promised, China would not have to choose between developing agriculture or industry. It could do both at the same time, or, as the slogan went, China could "walk on two legs." Mao admitted that his ambitious goals would take hard work, but it would be worth the effort. Unlike Winston Churchill, the British leader who at the beginning of World War II frankly promised his nation nothing but "blood, toil, tears, and sweat," Mao ecstatically prophesied "hard work for three years, happiness for a thousand." For openers, the Great Leap Forward would begin with a 100 percent jump in production of all goods within one year.

How could this incredible task be accomplished? Mao began, in theory at least, by taking one of China's disadvantages and turning it on its head to become an advantage. It was true, he admitted, that China was backward and had millions of wretchedly poor people. But, contrary to what most so-called experts asserted, that did not have to hold China down, he said:

> Apart from their other characteristics, China's 600 million people have two remarkable characteristics; they are, first of all, poor, and secondly blank. That may seem like a bad thing, but it is really a good thing. Poor people want change, want to do things, want revolution. A clean sheet of paper has no blotches, and so the newest and most beautiful words can be written on it, the most beautiful pictures can be painted on it.[4]

4. Stuart R. Schram, *The Political Thought of Mao Tse-tung* (New York: Praeger, 1963), p. 253.

The key was to tap into the energy and desire of those hundreds of millions of poor. If that could be done there was no limit to what the CCP could accomplish.

A variety of methods was used to release that energy. During late 1957 and early 1958, tens of millions of peasants were mobilized for a campaign to build water-control projects and other public works. There was also a mass campaign to wipe out what the party called the "four pests": flies, mosquitoes, rats, and sparrows. As part of the effort to "walk on two legs," officials and peasants at the local level were urged to build small-scale industries that could serve their needs. Another change was to remove factories from the control of central planners and turn them over to local authorities.

However, the real foundation of the Great Leap Forward was made up of what were called People's Communes. During a frenzied six-month period beginning in the spring of 1958, China's 750,000 collective farms, on which 500 million peasants had only recently been placed, were fused together into 26,000 communes. These new institutions were gigantic communities averaging about 25,000 people in each. A typical commune had 10,000 acres (4,000 hectares) of farmland—this in a country where before 1949 a typical peasant family farmed less than an acre. A commune also had over 100,000 farm animals, mainly chickens, cows, pigs, goats, and sheep. Intended to be self-sufficient communities, communes also contained children's nurseries, schools, industries, recreational facilities, and other services.

As gigantic as they were, what truly made the communes the springboard of Mao's Great Leap Forward was the way in which they were organized. Many Communist principles, which according to most Marxists could only be applied in the distant future, were introduced on the communes. Whereas on collective farms families had private plots and a few privately owned animals, these remnants of what Mao considered capitalism were eliminated on the communes. Consistent with Marx's slogan about communism, workers were paid according to their needs, not according to the work they did. Enormous mess halls were set up to replace individual family kitchens. The mess halls were intended to serve at least two functions. The CCP expected them to weaken family ties, which from the party's point of view were negative because they fostered loyalties that rivaled those of the revolution. In addition, along with the children's nurseries, the mess halls freed millions of women from their traditional domestic chores. This left them available to join the men as part of "work armies" in the fields or in other tasks outside the home. Family ties were attacked further by destroying individual peasant homes and forcing peasants to live in dormitories.

At the same time, the party introduced what it considered to be improved farming techniques. No longer would farmers work close to home in the fields they knew. They served instead in huge work teams that moved from one strange field to another over a large region. On party orders, crops were planted closer together on the theory that more plants per acre would increase the yield. Deep plowing, which was supposed to bring fertile soil to the surface, was another party innovation, as was the digging of thousands of wells to increase the water supply. Meanwhile, millions of peasants continued to be mobilized and taken far from their homes to labor on yet more public works projects.

The most distinctive symbols of the new Great Leap Forward were not, however, closely planted crops, deep furrows in the fields, or even public works projects. They were the "backyard steel mills," which sprang up all over China as part of the party's campaign to "walk on two legs" by developing small-scale industry. Over 600,000 of these homespun furnaces were built, to be manned by as many as 90 million peasants, workers, doctors, students, and other dedicated Chinese. Driven to a frenzy of enthusiasm by a massive propaganda campaign, they flocked to their makeshift mills after work, on weekends, and whenever else they could find the time. Determined to meet the CCP's call for more steel, they fed the hungry furnaces their family cooking pots and utensils, the hinges on their doors, and any other iron they could scrape up.

From Great Leap to Terrible Fall

Unfortunately, neither the music, the propaganda, nor anything else could turn overgrown fireplaces manned by amateurs into modern steel mills run by professionals. The steel they produced was useless. And its price was terribly high. Millions of people were left exhausted by the effort, which came on top of their regular jobs. Uncounted trees were cut down to fuel the backyard furnaces, leaving large areas deforested and subject to erosion and flooding. Tools that once enabled millions to earn their living were melted down into heavy junk.

The Great Leap Forward ended as one of the greatest disasters in China's long history. Laborers sent to distant work sites were not returned to their

Workers smelt steel at a "backyard steel mill," one of
thousands built during the Great Leap Forward.

own communes in time for the harvest. Suddenly and ironically, China's usually overpopulated countryside faced a critical labor shortage. Furthermore, work teams that moved from field to field in assembly-line fashion performed poorly. They lacked the vital personal knowledge a farmer normally has about how to best farm his field; they therefore often made costly mistakes. Nor did peasants laboring miles from home work carefully in fields whose harvest they would never see. And paying everyone equally regardless of the work done demoralized hard workers. In the end, equal pay for unequal work produced many more slackers who took advantage of the system than idealists who were inspired by it. Many of the new wells the party had ordered yielded no water, while others dug without proper planning ruined valuable pasturelands. Crops planted too close together did not grow. Deep plowing was no better, as one angry rice farmer pointed out:

> Before, the water in the [rice] paddy used to be above the ankle; now it went above the knee. But deep down the soil is no good, too compact. Only four to five inches [10 to 13 centimeters] on the surface are good. It wasn't correct but we couldn't help it. We got orders.[5]

Nor was killing pests always the best policy, especially if they were sparrows. In its determination to get rid of the sparrows and save the grain they ate, the party leadership forgot that sparrows also ate insects. Soon

5. Quoted in Alasdair Clayre, *The Heart of the Dragon* (Boston: Houghton Mifflin, 1985), p. 144.

swarms of those uneaten insects spread across the land, causing far more agricultural losses than any flocks of sparrows. The attacks on the family, from the dreary dormitories to the chaotic mess halls, angered the peasants, including the women the party insisted it was liberating from their traditional inferior roles.

Some of these problems were visible as early as late 1958. In December, the party therefore reversed some of its policies. More significantly, Mao was, at least partially, pushed aside. It was announced that Mao would retire as president of the PRC and that Liu Shaoqi would take his place. Mao still remained as party chairman, but losing the presidency removed him from many day-to-day decisions about running China. Mao was criticized again in July at a leadership meeting by Defense Minister Peng Dehuai, a heroic soldier widely admired in party circles. The chairman counterattacked fiercely, refusing to take the blame for the Great Leap's failures and reminding his audience that Marx also made many mistakes. He demanded that they continue the Great Leap, and warned that if they refused he would:

> . . . go to the countryside to lead the peasants to overthrow the government. If those of you in the Liberation Army won't follow me, then I will go and find a Red Army, and organize another Liberation Army. But I think the Liberation Army will follow me.[6]

Mao's counterattack worked. Peng was removed from his post, and the Great Leap was resumed in 1959.

6. Quoted in Maurice Meisner, *Mao's China: A History of the People's Republic* (New York: The Free Press, 1977), p. 245.

Peng, who was eventually arrested and died in prison for defying Mao, wrote a moving poem describing what he saw when he visited a commune in 1959 and what he feared was about to happen to his country because of Mao's fanaticism:

> Millet is scattered all over the ground.
> The leaves of the sweet potatoes
>   are withered.
> The young and the strong have gone
>   to smelt iron.
> To harvest the grain there are children
>   and old women.
> How shall we get through the next year?[7]

The terrible answer was that millions of Chinese did not get through the next several years. The grain harvest of 1958, while well below the initial glowing party reports, had reached 200 million tons, 25 million above 1957. But the disruption and disorganization of the Great Leap, as well as bad weather, caused the harvest to drop by more than 20 percent over the next two years. The Great Leap plunged China into the worst famine in human history. At least 25 million people died, double the number in the disastrous drought and famine of 1877–1879. Although the government tried with considerable success to suppress news of the disaster, refugees streaming out of China brought with them bits and pieces of the truth. An American journalist reported what some refugees told him:

7. Quoted in Roderick MacFarquhar, *The Origins of the Cultural Revolution*, vol. 2: *The Great Leap Forward*, 1958–1960 (New York: Columbia University Press, 1983), p. 200.

By late 1960, there was no meat, no fish, scarcely any vegetables, and reduced portions of rice. People spoke of having eaten wild herbs, of using a rancid rice-bran oil. A girl . . . said that peasants ate cakes made from cotton seeds, a form of nourishment normally reserved for pigs. A young man . . . described how raw rice was steamed twice so that the additional water would increase its weight and make the ration go farther.[8]

At the same time, industrial production plunged, leaving China mired in a maze of economic disaster and human tragedy.

The Sino-Soviet Split

China's problems during the Great Leap Forward were compounded by growing tensions with the Soviet Union that eventually produced a bitter split between the world's two most powerful Communist countries. Their relationship had been on shaky ground from the beginning, and that foundation was eroded further after the death of Joseph Stalin in 1953. Mao and Stalin had never gotten along very well, but Stalin's accomplishments as the man who industrialized the Soviet Union and led it through World War II had made him the undisputed leader of the Communist world. Mao

8. Stanley Karnow, "Why the Refugees Fled," in Franz Shurman and Orville Shell, eds., *Communist China: Revolutionary Reconstruction and International Confrontation, 1949–1966* (New York: Vintage Books, 1966), p. 462.

did not accord the same respect to Stalin's successor, Nikita Khrushchev. His attitude toward Khrushchev began to become hostile after 1956. In February, Khrushchev attacked Stalin in a famous speech at the 20th Congress of the Communist party of the Soviet Union in Moscow. Mao was angered because Khrushchev did not consult him, and also because many of Khrushchev's criticisms of Stalin—in particular that he built a personal dictatorship and inflated his accomplishments—could be applied to Mao as well.

Like many other Communist leaders, Mao blamed the anti-Communist Hungarian uprising of November 1956 on Khrushchev's speech. Mao also strongly disapproved of Khrushchev's attempt to improve relations with the United States, a policy Khrushchev called "peaceful coexistence." In particular, Mao was furious that Khrushchev and the Soviet Union did not support the PRC's attempt to drive Chiang Kai-shek's forces from two small islands in the Taiwan Straits. Mao also opposed Khrushchev's reforms inside the Soviet Union, which included an attempt to raise the Soviet standard of living, because he considered them capitalistic rather than socialist.

Khrushchev, in his turn, opposed and feared Mao's militant and unyielding anti-Americanism. The Soviet leader was especially appalled by Mao's nonchalant readiness to risk nuclear war in his struggle against American "imperialism." Mao's 1957 statement on the subject probably upset the Soviets as much as it did the Americans:

> Let us imagine, how many people would die if war should break out? Out of the world's population of 2,700 million, one third—or, if

more, half—may be lost. . . . If the worst came to the worst and half of mankind died, the other half would remain while imperialism would be razed to the ground and the whole world would become socialist; in a number of years there would be 2,700 million again.[9]

Worst of all for Chinese-Soviet relations, the Soviets opposed the Great Leap Forward, which they saw as a direct challenge to Soviet leadership of the Communist world. By 1959, the supposedly "unshakable unity" of the Communist world was coming apart at the seams. Khrushchev commented that China's communes could only have been set up by people who "do not properly understand what communism is or how it is to be built."[10] At the same time the Soviet Union ended its commitment to provide China with nuclear technology.

Matters went from bad to worse as the new decade began. In 1960, without warning, the Soviets stopped all aid and withdrew all their advisers from China, leaving almost three hundred projects unfinished. In 1962, the Chinese denounced Khrushchev for being a coward when he backed down in the face of overwhelming American power during the Cuban Missile Crisis. That same year, the Soviets returned the favor by siding with India when China fought and won a short but fierce border war with its large southern neighbor. And in 1963, when the Soviet Union signed a

9. Quoted in MacFarquhar, p. 10.
10. Quoted in Meisner, p. 245.

partial nuclear test ban treaty with the United States, the Chinese condemned both the Soviets and the treaty. By 1964, with Mao's denunciation of what he called Khrushchev's "phony communism," the gloves were completely off. Once allies, the world's two Communist giants had reached a parting of the ways. Khrushchev's fall from power in October did not stop the widening of the Sino-Soviet split.

Liu Shaoqi and the Return of Common Sense

At home, the Great Leap Forward provoked a far more serious split, this one within the CCP itself. Although Mao remained as party chairman after the Great Leap collapsed in 1960, the CCP turned away from his leadership. A group of more-flexible leaders headed by Liu Shaoqi and including Zhou Enlai, Chen Yun, and Deng Xiaoping took control of the country's day-to-day affairs. Liu was well suited to the task of leading the recovery effort. He was a brilliant organizer and workaholic whose history of successes dated from the 1920s. His reputation for honesty was sterling. And he lacked Mao's uncontrollable ego, which enabled Liu to admit that the Great Leap Forward had brought China to disaster. Still, not even Liu Shaoqi could turn things around instantly. From 1960 through 1962, China endured what its people would call the "three bitter years."

Liu began by focusing on feeding China's people. The communes, while officially left in place, were in practice broken down into smaller units. Often these units coincided with traditional villages. Peasants once again were paid according to work done, and their private plots were restored. Communal dining halls and similar disastrous and unpopular policies were abolished. In the cities, the central planners again took control of industry. At the same time, factory managers were allowed to introduce material incentives, such as paying workers according to what they produced. Liu put Deng Xiaoping in charge of demoting or removing party cadres who had advanced their careers on the basis of the Great Leap. Deng also restored to their posts many officials who had been purged during the "anti-rightist" campaign of 1957–1958.

Liu even permitted criticism of Chairman Mao, although without mentioning his name directly. In 1961, a play called *Hai Rui Dismissed from Office*, by writer Wu Han, appeared. The play was about a Ming dynasty emperor who unjustly dismissed a loyal servant from his post. The emperor in question bore an unmistakable resemblance to Chairman Mao, and the dismissed servant obviously was Peng Dehuai. It was equally clear as one read about the faults of the Ming ruler that Mao was being criticized for more than his treatment of Peng:

> You did a fairly good job in your early years, but what has happened to you now? . . . By suspecting court officials, you are mean to your subordinates. . . . The peasants begin to revolt everywhere . . . . Your shortcomings are numerous: rudeness, short-temperedness, self-righteousness, and deafness to honest criticism. But worst of all is your search for immortality. . . . The most urgent problems today are the absurdity of your imperial poli-

cies and the lack of clarity of official respon-
sibilities. If you do not tackle that problem
now, nothing will be accomplished.[11]

And in 1962, when Liu said that 70 percent of the
disasters of the GLF were due to human error and only
30 percent to natural causes, it was well understood
which party leader was to blame for that 70 percent.

By 1962, China was restored to economic health.
While hundreds of millions of Chinese greeted Liu's
success with relief and joy, Mao and his followers
brooded in the background. Mao did not like being out
of power, and he did not like Liu's policies. His frustra-
tion and his determination to reassert his power soon
brought China to yet another upheaval: the Great Proletarian Cultural Revolution.

11. Quoted in Edward E. Rice, *Mao's Way* (Berkeley: University of
California Press, 1974), p. 188.

THE CULTURAL
REVOLUTION

Between 1962 and 1965, an outward calm appeared to reign in the People's Republic of China. The big success story of that period was the country's economic performance. Liu Shaoqi and his colleagues continued their successful program of stressing economic recovery in general and improving agriculture in particular. Peasant production teams of twenty to thirty households were freed from stifling controls and were allowed to produce more goods for the free market on private plots. The government invested in irrigation machinery, factories to produce fertilizer, and other types of agricultural tools. This combination of targeted investment and common sense had returned agricultural production to its pre–Great Leap levels by 1965.

In the industrial sector, the government closed many inefficient factories and imported modern equipment—including entire factories—to increase

Workers wave copies of the "Little Red Book"—Quotations of Chairman Mao— at a mass rally in Beijing in 1966.

productivity. By 1965 industrial production was growing at the spectacular rate of 27 percent per year. As an added bonus, recent oil discoveries in Manchuria helped increase oil production by ten times and freed China from its reliance on Soviet oil. Overall, Liu seemed to be seeking a balance between fostering the party's goals of economic growth on the one hand, and simultaneously building socialism and improving the lives of the people on the other.

Liu's policies were unquestionably popular with people as far apart in status and location as peasants in remote areas and intellectuals in large cities. One intellectual probably expressed what hundreds of millions of his less literate countrymen felt when he wrote in his local newspaper:

> I think that happiness means leading a peaceful pleasant life, not a life of struggle and hardship. . . . It is strange logic to equate hardship with happiness and enjoyment of creature comforts with bourgeois thought.[1]

But the outward calm that made it possible to publish these comments covered a deeper turmoil. Mao Zedong did not agree with the letter writer's benign and passive view of life. The party chairman was convinced that what mattered above all else was that the people "never forget the class struggle." And that is precisely what he feared was happening in China. Mao called this straying from class struggle "revisionism," and warned that it could erode the revolution and bring China back to "capitalism." Mao pointed to the Soviet

1. Quoted in Merle Goldman, *China's Intellectuals: Advise and Dissent* (Cambridge, Mass.: Harvard University Press, 1981), p. 108.

Union in the post-Stalin era as an example of a country having betrayed its socialist revolution. That betrayal, Mao insisted, explained the Soviet Union's friendliness with the United States and its failure to support China against Taiwan and India.

Mao had several specific complaints about China under Liu's leadership. The chairman objected to what he called Liu's "capitalist" economic methods, which included everything from allowing peasants to have private plots, to paying factory workers according to what they produced. These practices would inevitably create richer and poorer people and hence class differences that were fundamental to capitalism but fatal for socialism. Mao argued that ends and means were inseparable. Socialist methods such as abolishing private plots would lead to socialism, while "capitalist" methods that made use of material incentives would put China on the "capitalist road." And the inequality Mao feared so greatly was even more pronounced when rural areas were compared with the cities. In urban factories, workers who used advanced machines earned twice as much as peasants who labored with their hands in the fields of the countryside.

Mao had an even more serious complaint about the CCP itself: It was changing and was losing its revolutionary spirit. The CCP Mao had built was long gone. No longer was it the closely knit group of comrades of the Yan'an days who lived simply and worked closely with the peasantry according to the principles of the mass line. In its place was a huge bureaucratic organization of 18 million people, most of whom had joined the party after 1949. For them the party was a source of advancement, privilege, and a good career. They had not suffered and sacrificed like the veterans of the Yan'an days. Making matters worse, even many of those veterans had grown comfortable in their post-1949 positions of authority.

Mao complained further that party members used their connections to pass on their privileges to their children. The children of the party elite, as well as those of nonparty urban intellectuals, went to the finest schools, which Mao and his supporters angrily called "little treasure pagodas." These children were the best equipped to meet the high standards for university admission, standards that Liu had made even more rigorous in 1961. What especially galled Mao was that this system reminded him of the old Confucian days, when China's educational system was designed to create an elite that would rule and control the people.

Mao called this tendency in the party "bureaucratism." He said it was creating a new "bourgeois" class, deliberately using the word that Marxists traditionally used to describe the ruling class under capitalism. In other words, China was in danger of repeating the same pattern that had undermined socialism in the Soviet Union. Early in 1962, Mao issued a direct and chilling warning at a large party conference:

> There are some bad people, bad elements and degenerate people who have infiltrated into our ranks, and degenerate elements who sit on the heads of the people. . . . We must find a way to deal with this type of people, and arrest some and execute a few of the worst who have committed the biggest crimes and greatest evils.[2]

2. "Talk at an Enlarged Central Work Conference," in Stuart Schram, ed., *Chairman Mao Talks to the People: Talks and Letters, 1956–1971* (New York: Pantheon Books, 1974) p. 184.

Liu Shaoqi and his supporters did not agree with Mao's grim forecast. At the same conference in which Mao warned about "bad elements," the party leadership rejected his defense of the Great Leap Forward and lined up with Liu, who bluntly called it a failure. In effect, by the early 1960s the CCP had two rival models of how to build socialism: Mao's and Liu's. Mao's approach relied on ideological correctness and mobilizing the enthusiasm of the masses. Liu's approach certainly did not ignore Marxism, but it also relied on practical policies Mao called "capitalistic" and on giving authority to experts who had the knowledge to solve technical problems. Because of this divergence, the dispute between the two camps was called the "Red Versus Expert" debate, with Mao and his fellow "Red" ideologues opposed to Liu and his "Experts." Over the next several years, this debate pulled the party apart until it had created a deep, wide, and ultimately unbridgeable split.

Mao Prepares His Comeback

Mao did more than simply criticize Liu and his policies. The chairman worked hard to find supporters, so that he could make a political comeback. One of those who were prepared to work tirelessly and fight hardest for Mao was his wife, Jiang Qing. Jiang had been an actress of limited talent prior to arriving in Yan'an and meeting Mao in the 1930s. Mao divorced his previous wife, a respected Long March veteran, to marry Jiang. Because of this, Jiang was never accepted by most of the old-time party leaders. Jiang remained removed from active politics until after the Great Leap, nursing a bitterness toward those who had rejected her.

Jiang Qing's specialty was culture. She expressed Mao's view, which has been held by Marxists and other political radicals since the nineteenth century, that art should serve political ends. Whether musicians, painters, poets, playwrights, or anything else, "good" artists were to use their creations not for self-expression but to deliver the correct political message. Mao himself had told his comrades in Yan'an:

> In the world today all culture, all literature, and art belong to definite classes and are geared to definite lines. There is in fact no such thing as art for art's sake, art that stands above classes or art that is detached from or independent of politics.[3]

With Mao's words in mind, Jiang in her first major speech complained about the state of culture in China with Liu in charge.

> Our operatic stage is occupied by emperors, princes, generals, ministers, scholars, and beauties. . . . The grain we eat is grown by the peasants, the clothes we wear and the houses we live in are all made by the workers, and the People's Liberation Army stands guard at the fronts of national defense for us and yet we do not portray them on the stage. . . .[4]

3. Quoted in Jack Gray and Patrick Cavendish, *Chinese Communism in Crisis* (London: Pall Mall, 1968), pp. 124–125.

4. Roxane Witke, *Comrade Chiang Ching* (Boston: Little, Brown, 1977), p. 362.

Besides relying on his wife, Mao counted heavily on several other dedicated supporters. Chen Boda, a former university professor, was a skilled propagandist who served as Mao's personal secretary with fanatical dedication. Kang Sheng, another supporter, was a truly sinister figure whose résumé included heading the PRC's secret police. His skill and ruthlessness had earned him the nickname "China's Beria," after Lavrenty Beria, Stalin's dreaded secret police chief. But most important of all was Lin Biao, China's minister of defense ever since Mao had purged Peng Dehuai in 1959. Lin was an outstanding soldier who had led CCP troops with great skill during the Long March, World War II, the civil war, and the Korean War. What made him so crucial was that as minister of defense he commanded China's People's Liberation Army (PLA), and in China there was considerable truth to Mao's dictum that "political power grows out of the barrel of a gun." By the early 1960s, Lin was busily fashioning the PLA into a Maoist stronghold. Mao's supporters were placed in key positions, and the entire PLA was inundated by pro-Mao propaganda. The soldiers were taught to:

> . . . read Chairman Mao's works, listen to his words, do as he instructs, and become a good soldier of Chairman Mao.[5]

They were told to emulate Lei Feng, a soldier who until his death in an accident had devoted his life to the revolution and quoting the thoughts of Chairman Mao.

5. Stephen Uhalley, Jr., A *History of the Chinese Communist Party* (Stanford, Calif.: Hoover Institution Press, 1988), p. 134.

Lei Feng's diary, conveniently discovered after his death, was the perfect vehicle for PLA troops to use in following Lin Biao's order to "Learn Resolutely from Comrade Lei Feng." The soldiers, of course, did not know that the diary was a forgery and had been written by the PLA propaganda department. Another PLA creation was authentic: a collection of snippets from Mao's writings and speeches called *Quotations of Chairman Mao*. Also known as the "Little Red Book" because of its small size and red cover, it was first published in 1963 and was distributed to millions of troops. Within a few years the book was literally everywhere in China. It became, in effect, a sacred text for hundreds of millions of Chinese striving to serve Chairman Mao.

Lin's value as Mao's ally grew with his achievements as minister of defense during the 1960s. The PLA's swift and decisive victory over India in the border war of 1962 added to his prestige. So did China's successful test of its first nuclear bomb in October 1964. Under the slogan "Learn from the PLA," Lin was able to extend its influence into civilian affairs. Military personnel, among other assignments, were involved in the "Socialist Education" anticorruption campaign of 1962–1965, were assigned to special political bureaus in schools and factories, and were active as officials in rural communes.

The Great Proletarian Cultural Revolution

The first shot of what exploded into the Cultural Revolution was fired in November 1965 when one of Mao's supporters attacked the play *Hai Rui Dismissed from Office* in a Shanghai newspaper. Aside from the play's unfortunate author, Wu Han, that shot was aimed at the longtime mayor of Beijing, Peng Zhen. Peng was a vocal critic of Mao and had supported both the play and its author. In the spring of 1966, Peng Zhen was removed from office. The announcement of the dismissal of a man of Peng's importance left no doubt as to what had become the worst sin a CCP member could commit:

> Anyone who opposes Chairman Mao Zedong opposes Mao Zedong's thoughts, opposes the central party leadership, opposes the proletariat's dictatorship, opposes the correct way of socialism. Whoever that may be, however high his position and however long his standing, he will be struck down by the entire party and the entire people.[6]

The new movement was officially announced to China and the world on April 18, 1966, when the PLA journal *Liberation Army Daily* called for a "cultural revolution." On April 30, Premier Zhou Enlai endorsed that call in the same journal:

> A socialist cultural revolution with a significant historical meaning is now rising in our country. This is a fierce and long-term struggle in the ideological sphere between the proletariat and the bourgeoisie. We have vigorously to promote proletarian thoughts and

6. Quoted in O. Edmund Clubb, *20th Century China*, 3d ed. (New York: Columbia University Press, 1978), p. 404.

smash bourgeois thoughts in all the academic, educational, journalistic, art, literary, and other cultural circles. . . . It is of the utmost importance, involving the fate and future of our Party and our country.[7]

The pace of activity picked up in May. A poster went up on May 25 at Beijing University denouncing its president for keeping students under control and calling for them "resolutely, thoroughly, totally, and completely to wipe out all monsters, demons, and all counterrevolutionary revisionists. . . ."[8] A few days later the first Red Guard unit was set up in a secondary school. The Red Guards were students, often teenagers, from China's secondary schools and universities. Many of them were the children of peasants and workers and therefore lacked the resources to succeed in China's highly competitive educational system. The Red Guards, whom the Maoists called their "little revolutionary generals," quickly spread to all the schools in Beijing, and from there to schools in cities across China. By the summer there were over 11 million of them. With the schools closed and with backing by the PLA, the Red Guards were free to lash out at what they called the "four olds"—old ideas, old culture, old customs, and old habits—and to otherwise do the bidding of their wise "supreme commander," Mao Zedong.

In July, a few days after Lin's PLA troops entered Beijing, the seventy-three-year-old Mao quashed rumors about his health by plunging into the Yangtze

7. Dick Wilson, *Zhou Enlai* (New York: Viking Press, 1984), p. 239.

8. Quoted in Stanley Karnow, *Mao and China* (New York: Viking Press, 1973), p. 174.

River and swimming for over an hour. On August 5 Mao spoke to his Red Guard fans in unmistakable terms when he put up a poster with the words *Bombard the Headquarters*. A week later, at a meeting of the party's Central Committee, Mao's position was strong enough to enable him to revamp the Politburo Standing Committee, the CCP's highest body, and take control of it. Although the meeting lacked a quorum, Mao had the Central Committee issue a statement about the impending Cultural Revolution. It would "sweep away all monsters," "touch men to their very souls," and "put daring above all else and boldly arouse the masses."[9] In another important power shift, Lin Biao moved into the party's number two slot as vice chairman and heir apparent to Mao, while Liu Shaoqi dropped to eighth in rank. Lin soon returned the favor to Mao with the following description of him in a new edition of the *Little Red Book*:

> Comrade Mao Zedong is the greatest Marxist-Leninist of our time. Comrade Mao Zedong has, with genius and in a creative and all-around way, inherited, defended, and developed Marxism-Leninism, advancing it to a completely new stage. . . . Once Mao Zedong's thought is mastered by the broad masses, it will become an inexhaustible source of strength and an infinitely powerful spiritual atom bomb.[10]

9. Quoted in Uhalley, p. 147.

10. Harold C. Hinton, ed., *The People's Republic of China, 1949–1979: A Documentary Survey*, vol. 3 (Wilmington, Del.: Scholarly Resources, 1980), p. 1460.

Red Guards on the march.

The summer's activities reached an emotional peak on August 18, 1966. Over one million Red Guards, wearing their distinctive armbands, packed Beijing's central Tiananmen Square for a rally. Wearing his own Red Guard armband, Chairman Mao greeted his ecstatic youthful followers. After the rally the worshipful praise for the chairman mounted as what critics called the "cult of Mao" continued to take shape. The official New China News Agency, announcing the intention to "smash the old world to smithereens," explained that Mao would lead the way to the "new world":

> Sailing the seas depends on the helmsman, the growth of everything depends on the sun, and making revolution depends on Mao Zedong's thought. . . . Chairman Mao is the reddest sun of our hearts.[11]

By the end of the month Lin Biao had perfected the formula for praising Mao. He was "our great teacher, great leader, great supreme commander, and great helmsman."[12]

Ten million Red Guards would come to Tiananmen Square for eight gigantic rallies during the next three months to see Chairman Mao. Those who missed him in 1966 got another chance of sorts on May 1, 1967. A Red Guard later described the scene:

> . . . we heard the great news: Chairman Mao was in the park. . . . we ran gasping to the spot, but it was too late. He was gone. All

11. Quoted in Witke, p. 325.
12. Quoted in Jonathan Spence, *The Search for Modern China* (New York: Norton, 1990), p. 605.

that remained of him was to touch the hands of the few who had been lucky enough to get close to him. But we didn't leave in disappointment. That trace of precious warmth in the palms of others seemed to us a more than adequate substitute for the real thing. Those Chairman Mao had touched now became the focus of our fervor. Everyone surged toward them with outstretched arms in hopes of transferring the sacred touch to their own hands. If you couldn't get close enough for that, then shaking the hand of someone who had shaken the hands of Our Great Saving Star would have to do. And so it went . . . until sometimes handshakes were removed as much as one hundred times from the original one. . . . The joy of touching the hand that had touched the hand that had touched the hand was indescribable, and there were tears in my eyes when I received the gift. . . .

The handshake didn't end there. All fourteen of us piled back into the truck and banged our drums and cymbals all the way back to the Central Institute of Music. . . . I must have stood there pumping for an hour. . . . I don't think it occurred to anyone that none of us had been anywhere near the man.[13]

Inspired by Chairman Mao, the Red Guards rampaged across China in the summer of 1966. They broke into

13. Liang Heng and Judith Shapiro, *Son of the Revolution* (New York: Vintage Books, 1983), p. 123.

the homes of "bourgeois," or "black," families, destroying paintings, books, and furniture and beating and torturing family members. They blazed a path of destruction through museums, temples, libraries, and historic buildings. They assaulted and murdered thousands of intellectuals, artists, teachers, administrators, party leaders, and even their own parents. Among those murdered was the distinguished author Lao She, whose moving novel *Cat Country* had protested the Chinese victimizing each other. Thousands more of China's most skilled and cultured people committed suicide or were imprisoned. Millions were uprooted from their homes and were sent to live in miserable conditions in the countryside. An enthusiastic Red Guard described what her group did to a historic mountain site near the city of Changsha, where for centuries people had gone to pray, burn incense, and admire China's rich past accomplishments:

> I was . . . trying to get rid of those old monuments and pavilions. And it wasn't an easy job, either. Half the stuff's made of stone. We had to use knives and axes to dig out the inscriptions. Stinking poetry of the feudal society. But it's all gone now, or boarded shut.[14]

Not even party leaders, many of whom were labeled "capitalist roaders" because they did not support Mao with sufficient enthusiasm, were safe from the Red Guards. They were paraded through the streets in dunce caps and were dragged into "struggle sessions"

14. Ibid., p. 70.

in front of thousands of spectators, where they were humiliated and beaten. Many were imprisoned under such terrible conditions that they died. Among those who were "struggled" was Wang Guangmei, Liu Shaoqi's wife and herself a prominent Communist. To mock and punish her for her stylish ways and her respect for Western culture, Wang was forced to wear a skintight silk gown, high-heeled shoes, and a necklace made of Ping-Pong balls. She was imprisoned, but she at least survived to hear her husband's reputation restored over a decade later. Liu Shaoqi was not so fortunate. After a lifetime of brilliant service to the CCP and its revolution, in 1968 he was expelled from the party and denounced as a "renegade, traitor, and scab" who had served the Guomindang. He died in prison in 1969 from pneumonia after neglect and cruel treatment. Deng Xiaoping, the party's general secretary when the Cultural Revolution had begun, was sent to a rural commune and managed to survive his ordeal physically intact. But he also knew permanent pain from the Cultural Revolution. His son, a respected scientist, was thrown out of a window by Red Guards and was left a paraplegic. As for the CCP as a whole, in most parts of the country its apparatus was shattered.

Even Zhou Enlai, who outwardly supported the Cultural Revolution but in fact tried to moderate it, found himself under attack. For a time he also found his task of running China's foreign policy made virtually impossible by the interference of the Red Guards. For example, during August 1967 they invaded and occupied China's foreign ministry. Shortly thereafter they ransacked the Soviet embassy. They also stormed and set fire to the British embassy, shouting "Kill! Kill!" and beating up a diplomat and tearing clothing off female employees. Needless to say, these and other incidents damaged China's relations with many countries.

While the Red Guards spearheaded the assault on Mao's opponents from below, Mao's wife Jiang Qing mounted her attack on China's culture from above. Jiang already had a reputation for fanaticism and viciousness when the Cultural Revolution began. As one official grimly commented, "When the old hen begins to crow at sunrise, the honorable farmyard is in danger."[15] And the Cultural Revolution was indeed Jiang's time to crow. On her orders, thousands of traditional Chinese plays, operas, and other works of art were banned, as was anything that smacked of Western influence. In their place were newly written plays, ballets, and operas delivering the identical politically correct message of heroic peasants, workers, and oppressed women routing evil "feudal" and "capitalist" forces. Some traditional works were even rewritten to deliver the same message.

As for China's genuine artists, poets, and musicians, they were unable to work and were often brutally mistreated. The distinguished pianist Liu Shikun was one of those who suffered terribly. As a prisoner of the Red Guards, he was denied the most minimal privacy to care for daily personal needs and was forced to sweep floors and clean toilets. His captors also taunted him with a song they made up:

> *Liu Shikun you bastard,*
> *Now you can surrender,*

15. Quoted in Craig Dietrich, *People's China* (New York and Oxford: Oxford University Press, 1986), p. 179.

If you do not tell the truth,
You may quickly die. . . .[16]

Ma Sitson, China's most famous violinist, was also seized by Red Guards. They not only beat him, but dumped paste on his head and forced him to wear a duncecap.

But all of these abuses paled next to what occurred in Guangxi Province in the southern part of the country. There Red Guards not only tortured and murdered, but actually ate their victims. In one incident, students killed school administrators and cooked their bodies in the school courtyard to prove their revolutionary spirit. The number of victims probably ran into the hundreds, and the number of cannibals into the thousands, in what was the largest incident of cannibalism in the world during the last one hundred years.

Education was yet another victim of the Cultural Revolution. When the schools and universities finally reopened after being closed for several months, old academic standards were abolished and many professors lost their positions. University admission suddenly depended on coming from the "correct" social class, which usually meant being the child of a peasant or of a worker. Politically correct subjects were emphasized—especially Mao Zedong Thought—and many traditional academic subjects were dropped. Examinations were rejected because they were supposedly "bourgeois" and were designed to keep down the children of the working masses. This approach to education gave a brief place in the sun to those who previously had been unable to succeed in China's tra-

16. Quoted in Liang and Shapiro, p. 121.

*Children at a Chinese kindergarten fire their
toy guns at a picture of an American in 1966.
During the Cultural Revolution, schools focused
on politics at the expense of education.*

ditional system. But by the 1980s, when the Cultural
Revolution was a thing of the past and China again
valued competent graduates with useful skills, the students of the late 1960s and 1970s had nothing to offer.
They became known as the "lost generation," while
younger people educated under a system of restored
academic standards pushed them aside and passed
them by.

As the Cultural Revolution drove China to the edge of anarchy, its economic progress ground to a halt and slipped into reverse. Industrial production dropped drastically. Foreign trade fell. Agricultural production suffered less, since the Cultural Revolution did most of its damage in the cities and often did not reach the vast and remote countryside. However, many peasants suffered when they were forced to give up their private plots and farm animals on which they had depended to maintain a minimal standard of living. Overall, economic production may have dropped by as much as 15 percent.

One activity that was given complete shelter from the Cultural Revolution storm was China's nuclear research program. There were several successful nuclear tests, culminating in the explosion of China's first hydrogen bomb in 1967. Three years later, the PRC demonstrated its rocketry skill by launching its first satellite.

Eventually Mao was forced to bring the Cultural Revolution to a halt. Early in 1967, Mao and Lin Biao had intervened in Shanghai to remove a group of ultra-radicals from power. A few months later, troops had to be sent to the industrial city of Wuhan to restore order. Near civil war raged in other areas as well, including Guangzhou, from which bodies thrown in the river floated down to Hong Kong every day. In the fall of 1967, Mao took his first steps to control the Red Guards by ordering the PLA to use force against them if necessary. However, the Cultural Revolution was not over, and violence and turmoil increased again during 1968. Some of the street battles were fought with heavy weapons such as tanks and artillery.

By the middle of 1968, however, Mao knew he had to end the turmoil. The chaos had gone too far and threatened China with complete anarchy. Added to this was the fact that Mao was increasingly afraid of the Soviet Union. In August 1968, the Soviets sent shock waves around the world when they invaded Czechoslovakia because they opposed a reform movement in that Eastern European Communist nation. In addition, a long-standing Sino-Soviet border dispute continued to fester. Mao therefore took decisive steps to wind down the Cultural Revolution during the second half of the year. When necessary, the army was used to disband the Red Guards and send them home. At its Ninth Party Congress, in April 1969, the CCP officially ended the Cultural Revolution. In its wake, 500,000 people were dead and as many as 100 million had seen their lives seriously disrupted and even ruined. While the worst was over, difficult times still lay ahead.

Mao's Last Hurrah

Although the Cultural Revolution itself ended in 1969, Mao and his supporters continued many of its policies in modified form until the chairman's death in 1976. So the era of the Cultural Revolution may be said to date from 1966 to 1976, which is why Mao's critics in China often refer to it as the "Ten-Year Catastrophe."

One area, however, in which there was great improvement after 1969 was foreign policy. A month before the April meeting that ended the Cultural Revolution, Chinese troops along the Russian border provoked a bloody armed clash. Other dangerous border incidents followed. Fear of the Soviet Union forced the Chinese to turn to the one country capable of standing up to the world's Communist superpower:

the United States. At the time the United States was in the process of withdrawing its army from South Vietnam. Across the sea, the world's greatest capitalist power increasingly seemed less of a threat to China than the world's greatest Communist power directly to the north.

By 1971, relations had improved dramatically, and a high-ranking American official secretly visited Beijing that summer. In October, the United States dropped its long-standing opposition to the PRC's entering the United Nations. Beijing took over the seat that Taiwan's nationalist regime had held in both the General Assembly and the Security Council, and Taiwan was expelled from the United Nations. Then, in 1972, President Richard Nixon, a lifelong anti-Communist, visited the PRC, where he immediately hit it off with Mao Zedong, a lifelong anticapitalist. At a banquet in his honor, Nixon toasted his hosts by quoting none other than Chairman Mao when he urged both sides to "seize the time" to build peaceful relations. The PRC's new openness and moderation soon brought the additional benefits of increased trade with the Western industrialized powers.

Ironically, the most serious conflict Mao had to face in his final years was at home. His opponent was none other than his presumed disciple and successor Lin Biao. The two men apparently differed over a variety of issues, among them the influence of the People's Liberation Army. In the process of ending the Cultural Revolution, the PLA had intervened in many areas of Chinese life, and this had enormously increased Lin's power. Mao therefore began to rebuild the shattered Communist party apparatus in order to counterbalance Lin's PLA. This required that many party officials

Zhou Enlai and Richard Nixon review Chinese troops during the U.S. president's historic 1972 visit.

purged during the Cultural Revolution be restored to their posts, a task Mao placed in Zhou Enlai's capable hands. Lin strongly opposed this, as well as Mao's diplomatic gesture to the United States. A struggle for power began. It ended in September 1971 when Lin tried to overthrow Mao. When his coup failed, Lin and several supporters fled the country in an air force jet that crashed in Outer Mongolia; all aboard the aircraft were killed.

After his fall, Lin was viciously attacked in the press. The militant radical who had supposedly been Mao's "closest comrade-in-arms" was suddenly transformed into a "closet Confucianist," "bourgeois careerist," and, of all things, an "ultra-rightist."

Lin Biao's demise ended one political storm, but China's political waters remained turbulent. With Mao's health worsening, the question of succession was on everyone's mind. Two main opposing factions existed within the party. The radical group was led by Jiang Qing. She and her three main allies, whom together Mao had called the "Gang of Four," militantly supported the Cultural Revolution policies. The moderate faction was grouped around Zhou Enlai, but he also was old and in failing health. Zhou's most important assistant was Deng Xiaoping, whom Zhou had brought back from political exile and restored to the party leadership in 1973. Deng immediately worked to restore to their posts as many officials purged during the Cultural Revolution as possible. A third faction stood between the radicals and the moderates. Its leading member was Hua Guofeng, an official from Mao's native Hunan Province who was of minor importance except for the support he received from Chairman Mao.

The End of the Mao Zedong Era

Zhou Enlai died on January 8, 1976. When a large crowd gathered in Tiananmen Square during a traditional period of mourning in April, radicals loyal to Jiang interfered. A riot resulted in which hundreds were killed. Thousands of arrests followed, and Deng Xiaoping, whom Mao still distrusted as an unreformed Liuist, was again purged from office. Although Jiang and her extreme radical faction appeared to be in a strong position, Mao also did not trust them entirely. He put a roadblock in their way when he designated Hua Guofeng as his successor. The chairman even wrote to Hua, "With you in charge, I am at ease."

Mao died on September 9, 1976, at the age of eighty-three. His death ended one of the most tumultuous eras in China's long history. But it did not end the tumult in China. The CCP was deeply divided between supporters and opponents of the Cultural Revolution. Bitter rivals for power were poised to pounce and were waiting just out of sight in the shadows. The struggle for China's future was far from over.

CHINA UNDER DENG XIAOPING

Mao's death in September 1976 was followed by two successive struggles for power. The first was sudden and short. It pitted Jiang Qing and her partners in the Gang of Four against most of the other leaders in the CCP. The Gang of Four had prepared to seize power in a military coup, but Hua Guofeng beat them to the punch. He had no trouble lining up support, since both Jiang herself and her fanatically radical views were thoroughly unpopular and were greatly feared. Aided by top PLA commanders, leading Politburo members, and supporters of Deng Xiaoping, who himself was in hiding, Hua arrested the Gang of Four during the pre-dawn hours of October 6, just before Jiang herself was preparing to strike. Her protest when she was arrested—"How can you rebel when the chairman's body

1. Quoted in Immanuel C. Y. Hsü, *China Without Mao: The Search for a New Order*, 2d ed. (New York and Oxford: Oxford University Press, 1990), p. 18.

is not yet cold?"[1]—was of no help to her. By "smashing the Gang of Four," Hua Guofeng was doing what most Chinese wanted done.

Jiang and her associates were accused of many crimes, including persecuting or killing over 34,000 people. However, divisions within the party delayed their trial until the autumn of 1980. Jiang was accused of being the group's ringleader, and her conduct at the trial supported that charge. At age sixty-seven facing a battery of thirty-five hostile judges and having endured four years of solitary confinement, Jiang was fiercely unbowed. While her co-conspirators sat glum and silent, Jiang Qing, the former actress, gave the performance of her career. Defiantly she told her accusers:

> Fine. Go ahead! You can't kill Mao—he is already dead—but you can kill me. Still I regret nothing. I was right. . . . I dare you to sentence me to death in front of one million people in Tian An Men Square.[2]

Jiang went on to say, not without justification, that she was under attack because the party leadership did not dare to attack Mao directly. Or, as she put it rather crudely, their purpose was "to make me stink, and through me make Chairman Mao stink. . . ."[3] In the end, Jiang Qing, Mao's wife of thirty-eight years, had to be dragged from the courtroom, still shrieking at her judges. She and two other Gang of Four members were sentenced to death. The fourth was given a life sen-

2. Ibid., p. 137.

3. Perry Link, ed., *Stubborn Weeds: Popular and Controversial Literature After the Cultural Revolution* (Bloomington: Indiana University Press, 1983), p. 434.

tence, while several other conspirators in Jiang's planned coup, including Mao's former secretary Chen Boda, received long prison terms. None of the condemned were executed, however, probably because the government did not want to turn them into martyrs. Jiang committed suicide in prison in 1991.

The defeat of Jiang and the Gang of Four in 1976 did not settle the issue of who would rule China or what kind of policies China would follow in the years to come. Hua Guofeng was both chairman of the CCP and premier of the PRC, but he was a newcomer to China's political elite and lacked political clout. With Jiang and her cohorts gone, Hua represented Maoism and policies associated with Mao that had caused great suffering. By early 1977, Hua had to bow to widespread pressure and restore Deng Xiaoping to a position of leadership in the party. By the middle of the year, Deng had been restored to all of his former posts, including that of party vice chairman and chief of the general staff of the PLA. All of these factors made Hua vulnerable. He and his supporters tried to use Mao's reputation as the leader of the Communist revolution in China to prop themselves up. Early in 1977, a newspaper they controlled told the Chinese people:

> Let us hold still higher Chairman Mao's great banner and implement Chairman Mao's revolutionary line still more consciously. We resolutely defend whatever policies Chairman Mao has formulated and unswervingly adhere to whatever instructions Chairman Mao has issued. . . .[4]

4. Harold C. Hinton, ed., *The People's Republic of China, 1949–1979: A Documentary Survey*, vol. 4 (Wilmington, Del.: Scholarly Resources, 1980), pp. 2655–2656.

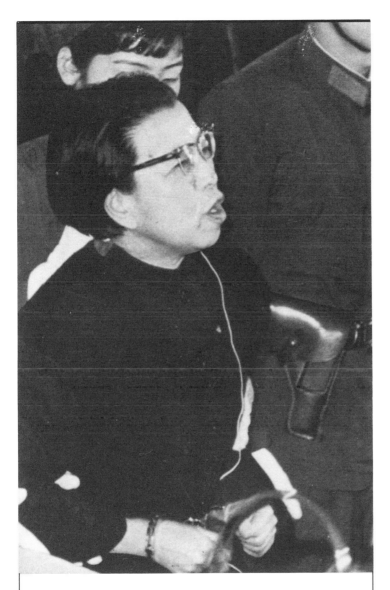

*A handcuffed Jiang Qing shouts defiantly at
the court after being sentenced to death.*

Hua's "two whatevers," as the references to Mao's policies and instructions were sarcastically called, were little help in the struggle against Deng. Neither was Hua's use of visual effects—the huge posters in which Hua's hairstyle and clothing were chosen to make him look like Mao. Gradually, Deng's power grew and Hua's declined. Signs of the changing times in 1977 included dropping Cultural Revolution bans on Beethoven's music and Shakespeare's plays and the restoration of university entrance exams. Although Hua was allowed to linger in office a while longer, by the end of 1978 Deng Xiaoping and his supporters were in charge.

The stage was set for a drastic change in policy, and reforms did in fact begin in 1978. However, before those reforms could go very far, Deng and his supporters had to do precisely what Jiang Qing at her trial had said they dared not do: directly challenge the legend of Mao Zedong. In order to justify major changes, China's new rulers had to discredit the policies of Mao with which they disagreed. This in turn required that Mao's reputation as a perfect, larger-than-life leader be cut down to size. At the same time, Mao's reputation could not be damaged too much, since that would undermine both the CCP and its new leadership under Deng.

Criticism of Mao began to be heard late in 1978. At a party meeting in December, the economist Chen Yun, who had unsuccessfully opposed Mao's Great Leap Forward, criticized Mao with a touch of bitter sarcasm:

> Had Chairman Mao died in 1956 [before the
> Great Leap Forward], there would have been

5. Quoted in Roger Garside, *Coming Alive: China After Mao* (New York: McGraw-Hill, 1981), p. 206.

no doubt that he was a great leader of the Chinese people. . . . Had he died in 1966 [before the Cultural Revolution], his meritorious achievements would have been somewhat tarnished, but his overall record still very good. Since he actually died in 1976, there is nothing we can do about it.[5]

Chen's comments, however blunt, were made at a closed meeting of the party elite, not to China as a whole. The public assessment of Mao did not come until June 1981, when the CCP announced its "Resolution on Certain Questions in the History of Our Party Since the Founding of the People's Republic." The resolution praised Mao for his leadership until 1956 and said that his "Thought" should continue to lead the party. However, it rejected his policies after that date, specifically the Great Leap Forward and the Cultural Revolution. The latter, in particular, "led to domestic turmoil and brought catastrophe to the party, the state, and the whole people."[6] Obviously, the time had come for new and profoundly different policies.

The Four Modernizations
of Deng Xiaoping

Deng's program differed so fundamentally from the Maoist vision that it has been called China's "second revolution." In effect, the second revolution was a departure from both the Maoist and Liuist models for building a new China. Deng rejected Maoist reliance

6. Quoted in Hsü, p. 148.

on human will and ideological purity as well as Liu's tendency to follow the Soviet example and make only limited use of nonsocialist policies. China's new leader called his program the "Four Modernizations," which referred to new approaches to agriculture, industry, science and technology, and national defense. After years of failed Maoist experiments, Deng was looking for policies that worked. As he once put it in a phrase that had infuriated Mao, "It does not matter if a cat is black or white, as long as it catches mice." In 1978 Deng put it another way: The time had come to "seek truth from facts." His goal was extremely ambitious: to quadruple China's gross national product by the year 2000 and turn China into a modern socialist state that gave most of its people a satisfactory standard of living.

As it had done just after seizing power almost thirty years earlier, the CCP began its reforms with agriculture. Between 1978 and 1984, China's 50,000 huge communes were broken up into individual family farms. Although the state retained legal ownership of the land, peasants were allowed to lease their land for long periods. They could pass these leases on to their children, hire laborers, and buy machinery. After delivering a certain amount of crops to the state, the peasants were able to produce and sell as they pleased according to market prices. They could specialize in activities such as raising farm animals, and could even go into business that provided necessary services in their region, such as repairing machinery, providing transportation to get crops to market, or painting houses. In other words, less than three decades after Mao had led the drive to put China's peasants on collective farms, the CCP under Deng's leadership abandoned collectivized agriculture.

Decollectivization produced impressive results. Agricultural output soared during the 1978–1988 decade at an annual rate of 6.2 percent. China was transformed from a country in which 150 million people lived on the verge of starvation to a nation able to feed itself and even export grain. While most peasants continued to use the old backbreaking methods of farming, some were able to make use of machinery and chemical fertilizers to increase their yields. New peasant businesses prospered; by 1988 nonagricultural rural businesses employed a fifth of the rural labor force. A popular slogan of the day was, "To get rich is glorious." And many peasants did, at least by Chinese standards. Their average income tripled between 1978 and 1984. They built new homes and furnished them with televisions and refrigerators, appliances that were virtually unheard of under Mao. In 1984 a group of fifty successful peasants began a three-month tour of Japan, a first for China. That same year a peasant in Hunan Province who had prospered by setting up a fertilizer and pesticide company became the first Chinese peasant to buy his own aircraft. A foreign observer witnessed the change over several visits to a province in southern China:

> When I first visited . . . in 1979, there was virtually nothing in the market. When I went back in 1981, things had started to pick up. But when I went back in 1983, I couldn't believe what I saw. There were hundreds of people selling things. There were tanks of live fish, and piles of fruit and vegetables heaped up everywhere. Lots of pigs were being slaughtered for meat—something you

rarely saw in the past. You could buy Coca-Cola, Budweiser beer, and foreign cigarettes in private shops. The prosperity was impressive.[7]

Deng's industrial reforms were also far-reaching. Individuals and collectives were permitted to operate state-owned factories and could also set up their own businesses. Unlike in the past, the collectives that ran these factories and businesses were not under state control. Some of them ran large businesses such as hotels or trading companies. Many new industrial enterprises were in rural areas, where they produced goods for the local market. As a result, the output of rural industry soared by 262 percent between 1982 and 1986.

Even more successful were the five so-called Special Economic Zones that were established along China's southwest coast. These zones were set up to attract foreign investment, and with it, advanced foreign technology. Foreign firms were permitted to operate free of most controls and regulations that applied in the rest of China. Within ten years after being set up in 1980, the zones had attracted over $4 billion in foreign investment. Foreigners built some of China's most competitive industries, and by 1990 factories in the zones accounted for a tenth of China's total exports.

This progress stood in contrast to the state-owned heavy industries in the cities that had been built under the five-year plans. Despite attempts to

7. Orville Shell, *To Get Rich Is Glorious*, rev. and updated ed. (New York: New American Library, 1986), p. 54.

give managers more authority and independence, the straitjacket of state control and policies from the past kept them operating inefficiently and often at a loss.

Deng also made progress in his two other modernizations: science and technology and national defense. Under Mao's leadership, specialists trained abroad had always been under suspicion and were subject to persecution in various campaigns, including the Cultural Revolution. Deng reversed these policies and gave these experts important posts. Standards were raised in China's schools and universities, and many students were sent abroad to study. China also turned to foreign advisers and consultants, including foreign governments, to help it master modern technology. Modernization of the military stressed advanced weapons and training while cutting down the size of the enormous military machine.

These impressive results, however, also had a negative side. In agriculture, grain production leveled off after 1987 as peasants switched to more-profitable products. Individual peasant farmers did not have the resources or time that the old communes did to care for public works such as flood-control projects. As a result, soil erosion increased. To enable their children to work the land, peasant families stopped sending them to school, sacrificing the children's future for current profits. Even worse, China's attempts to control its population were set back. When peasants were part of communes and fields were worked collectively, families had less need for additional children. However, the return to family farms had increased the need for cheap "hands" to work the fields. Because of this, rural peasant families increasingly violated the government's birth-control policies. In addition, the return to family farms created poor peasants as well as rich ones. This, in effect, broke the central promises of the 1949 revolution: that China would be a society in which wealth would be distributed equally.

In the cities, the rise in prices that came with a free market in agriculture hurt millions of urban workers on fixed wages. These included workers in state-run factories and salaried government and party employees. For example, in 1988, when controls were lifted on pork, vegetables, and sugar, their prices jumped by 30 to 60 percent. The lack of controls in factories in the Special Economic Zones led to horrendous working conditions. Particularly shocking were conditions involving children. Some factories violated Chinese law by employing children as young as ten. Other children slept two to three in a bed in dormitories after working fifteen-hour days. But they were luckier than the teenage girls who worked twenty-four-hour shifts. To many Chinese, these dreadful conditions recalled the bad days of the nineteenth and early twentieth centuries when foreign powers exploited a helpless China, times and conditions that the CCP was supposed to have ended forever in 1949.

Furthermore, as the government loosened its totalitarian grip on many areas of Chinese life, crime escalated as people with little or nothing to lose scrambled for a place in the sun. Some crimes, such as theft and embezzlement, were purely economic. Others involved assault, murder, rape, kidnapping, and other acts of violence. And many government officials used their positions to enrich themselves by accepting bribes from foreigners doing business in China. Deng's regime responded much as Mao's had in the past: swiftly and brutally. The first reaction came in 1983, when thousands of alleged criminals were rounded up and, without a chance to defend themselves legally, summarily executed. Many of the executions took place in public. A young man explained to a shocked foreign journalist why China's government did in public what other countries did only in private:

> They want to scare people and make a point. There's an old custom here in China, and they've revived it again. After a criminal has been shot, his family is sent a bill of twenty-five cents for the bullet. It's a reminder that a criminal not only brings punishment on himself but shame on the whole family in which he was raised.[8]

The Fifth Modernization and Tiananmen Square

Almost immediately after Deng began his Four Modernizations, he was confronted by the demand for a "Fifth Modernization": democracy. The demand was made in early 1979 in a poster put up at a place called "Democracy Wall" in Beijing, actually a wall near Beijing's main bus station. Deng had permitted Democracy Wall, and other sites like it elsewhere in China, to exist as long as the protests it carried were directed against Mao and the Cultural Revolution. Wei Jingsheng, the young man who put up the Fifth Modernization poster, asserted that only with democracy could China genuinely modernize. Without democracy, that

8. Ibid., p. 48.

People stop to read wall posters along a Beijing street. Posters calling for democracy led to a government crackdown in 1979.

goal would be unfulfilled, "all pledges by any Great Man to the contrary notwithstanding."[9] Another Wei poster, entitled "Do We Want Democracy or Dictatorship?", accused Deng of being a dictator.

Deng quickly answered Wei's challenge, demonstrating in the process that he and his fellow CCP leaders had already chosen between democracy and dictatorship. Wei Jingsheng was arrested, condemned as a "counterrevolutionary," and sentenced to fifteen years in prison under extremely harsh conditions that soon ruined his health. Democracy Wall was shut down. A general crackdown on intellectuals, with widespread arrests, followed. In March 1979, the same month he arrested Wei Jingsheng, Deng announced that henceforth China would operate according to "four basic principles" that would be above criticism: socialism, dictatorship of the proletariat, leadership of the Communist party, and what he called "Marxism-Leninism-Mao Zedong Thought." In 1983, the regime launched an "Anti–Spiritual Pollution" campaign against Western influences. But with thousands of Chinese students studying abroad, where they were exposed to Western ideas, and thousands of foreigners in China, Deng could not end talk about the Fifth Modernization. Low-level activity and protests continued until December 1986, when thousands of students in several cities openly demonstrated for democracy with slogans such as "No democracy, no modernization." Many were inspired by the words of Fang Lizhi, an astrophysicist and one of China's most brilliant

9. James D. Seymour, *China: The Fifth Modernization: China's Human Rights Movement, 1978–1979* (Stanfordville, N.Y.: Human Rights Publishing Group, 1980), p. 63.

scientists, who had courageously been speaking out for human rights in his country. Fang had also called Marxism obsolete and had pointed out that the CCP's rule in China was based on military conquest, not on the free consent of the people. He called for a "more open society, where differences are allowed."[10] The students were also able to read an even stronger attack on communism from one of China's leading journalists, Liu Binyan, who wrote:

> What is the essence of extreme leftism? It is mutual spite, mutual destruction, and mutual cruelty. . . . It makes a free man unfree. It makes a free personality into a submissive tool. It turns man into a beast. . . . Hence, I must submit that the essence of leftism is inhumanism.[11]

Arrests and the pressure to do well on examinations ended these demonstrations without a major incident. However, they ended the political career of the man Deng had promoted to the post of party general secretary, Hu Yaobang, a vigorous, efficient, and popular advocate of reform.

Still, the demands for political reform and democracy were not entirely silenced despite another offensive against foreign ideas in 1987 known as the "Anti-Bourgeois Liberalization" campaign. The tension between the CCP dictatorship and China's students and

10. Quoted in Jonathan Spence, *The Search for Modern China* (New York: Norton, 1990), p. 723.

11. Ibid., p. 216.

intellectuals came to a head in early 1989 in Tiananmen Square, where forty years earlier Mao Zedong had proclaimed the founding of the PRC. By April 1989, when the demonstration began, the Communist world, from the Soviet Union into Eastern Europe, was being swept by the reforms of Soviet leader Mikhail Gorbachev. Millions of Chinese students and intellectuals hoped that the wave of reform would surge over the Great Wall and into their country.

The demonstrations began modestly enough when three thousand students gathered in Tiananmen Square to mourn Hu Yaobang, who had died of a heart attack. Students renewed the call for democracy, with some beginning a hunger strike to back their demands. The students also denounced corruption in the CCP. One of their most popular slogans was "Sell the Benzes [Mercedes-Benz automobiles] and Pay the National Debt." The demonstrators also openly criticized China's hard-line premier, Li Peng, and even Deng himself, calling for their resignations. The students struck a deep chord of discontent, for the numbers of demonstrators swelled into the hundreds of thousands. Shocked and unprepared, Deng and the party leadership hesitated.

As the demonstration grew, drawing increasing support from all levels of Chinese society, it quickly became an international media event. Journalists from all over the world interviewed student leaders and transmitted words and pictures from Tiananmen Square across the globe. In the middle of May, Soviet leader Mikhail Gorbachev arrived for a three-day state visit, the first by a Soviet leader in thirty years. Because of the demonstration in Tiananmen Square, Gorbachev's official reception had to be moved. This further embarrassed and infuriated the Communist Party leadership.

The high point for the prodemocracy forces, and the low point for the CCP leaders, probably came on May 30. On that day students set up what they called their "Goddess of Democracy," a 30-foot (9-meter) statue closely resembling the Statue of Liberty. As the Goddess of Democracy stared directly at China's old Imperial Palace and a gigantic portrait of Chairman Mao, the democratic ideals of the West literally stood face-to-face with both the ancient and modern authoritarian traditions of China.

By this time Deng had decided to strike back, and strike back hard. He had removed the most outspoken reformer among the party leaders, General Secretary Zhao Ziyang, from his post and had declared martial law. On the night of June 3–4, PLA troops and tanks rolled through the streets of Beijing and charged into Tiananmen Square, deliberately shooting down unarmed students and other civilians in their path. There were some remarkable, although futile, acts of heroism, including a lone man standing in front of a column of tanks and temporarily forcing it to halt. The unforgettable picture of one man standing up to a convoy of military armor captured the admiration of the world, but it could not help the students in Tiananmen Square. Nor could the plea of Shen Tong, a student leader, who screamed out the bitter irony of what the soldiers were doing:

> Don't you know you're in Beijing? You are on Changan Avenue. Do you know the history of Changan Avenue? In 1949, when the People's Liberation Army liberated the city from the

*Demonstrators and news photographers crowd
around the "Goddess of Democracy" set up
by students in Beijing's Tiananmen Square at
the height of the 1989 demonstrations there.*

Guomindang, no shots were fired on Changan Avenue. When the foreign armies invaded Beijing, no one was killed on Changan Avenue. You are the People's Liberation Army and you're shooting your own people.[12]

No one knows how many people were killed or injured on the day the students called "Bloody Sunday," since the army was ordered to burn the bodies of the victims.

The massacre was followed by a massive manhunt and a wave of arrests. Hundreds of people were executed. Thousands of others disappeared into the *laogoi*, the vast network of three thousand prison labor camps where ten million people toil under brutal conditions. Many people were fired from their jobs because they were considered politically unreliable. The regime also tried to block Western broadcasts and printed materials from reaching the country. Although martial law was lifted in 1990, the next year saw a surge in repression and arrests.

The foreign reaction to the Tiananmen Massacre was minimal. None of the industrialized powers that might have put pressure on China were willing to damage their profitable economic ties with Beijing. A few temporary economic penalties and some restrictions on military sales added up to nothing more than a slap on the wrist. Agreements that were important to the PRC, such as the 1984 Chinese-British treaty under which Hong Kong would return to Chinese control in 1997, were not affected.

12. Shen Tong, *Almost a Revolution* (Boston: Houghton Mifflin, 1990), p. 324.

China in the 1990s

The pattern established during the 1980s—economic reform combined with political repression—continued into the 1990s. China's economy maintained its strong growth. Foreign investors from Hong Kong, Taiwan, South Korea, Japan, and, to a lesser extent, the United States and Europe continued to build new factories in China. China's exports of toys, shoes, clothing, and electronics products continued to surge. By 1992, its economy was growing by about 12 percent per year and was the third largest overall in the world, trailing only those of the United States and Japan. Of course, China's per capita income remained only a small fraction of that of the world's modern industrialized nations.

At the same time, rapid economic growth continued to exact its high price. Inflation was dangerously high. While prosperity had come to many Chinese, it was distributed unequally. Entire regions populated by hundreds of millions of people lagged behind. For example, the per capita income in landlocked and poverty-stricken Guizhou Province was only one sixth that of the bustling port of Shanghai. In general, as Deng's reforms led to large investments in urban areas, income in rural areas dropped to less than half that in cities. About 25 percent of the workforce lacked permanent jobs, so tens of millions of people migrated from place to place looking for work. At times, economic hardship led to open protests despite governmental repression. In June 1993, for example, peasants in Sichuan Province in central China rioted over high taxes. At one point ten thousand peasants attacked government offices, a dangerous sign for a regime that based its revolution on the peasantry.

At the other end of the economic spectrum was a small group of well-connected people and entrepreneurs who became extremely rich under Deng's economic reforms and who enjoyed flaunting their wealth. The wealthiest of them were about three thousand children of top party officials. They earned thousands of times more than the average Chinese, which is why they were sarcastically and angrily called the *tanzidang*, or "princelings." Despite these gross inequalities, the CCP leadership insisted it was building what it called a "socialist market economy." However, China's people were seeing less and less "socialism" and more and more "market" as its economy increasingly resembled the capitalist system the Communist revolution had supposedly overthrown. The wide-open economy also generated corruption, such as a $175 million swindle in China's new stock and bond markets in which 100,000 investors were defrauded.

Breakneck industrial growth also created severe pollution. In 1991, factories dumped 25 billion tons of waste into China's waterways, and acid rain caused by air pollution did $2.8 billion in damage to crops, forests, and buildings. In many cities, the air pollution levels were five to six times the standards set by the World Health Organization. Their residents often wore surgical masks when they ventured outside.

Rapid economic growth was not the only successful policy that came with a high price tag. So did the unrelenting campaign to limit the growth of China's population, which reached 1.17 billion in 1993. The good news was that by 1993 the average Chinese woman was expected to have 1.73 children in her lifetime, a birthrate comparable to that of modern industrialized countries. At that rate, China's population would peak at 1.9 billion in the mid-twenty-first century and would then finally begin to decline. However, the price of bringing down the birthrate so drastically included forced abortions and harsh punishments, including the destruction of their homes, for families who violated government directives.

A particularly terrible cost was borne by baby girls. The government's effort to limit families to one or two children clashed with China's ancient preference for boys to carry on the family line. In many cases, the birth of a girl was not recorded so that the new parents could try again for a boy. This means that hundreds of thousands of girls born each year do not officially exist and will be denied an education and other basic services. In other cases, pregnant women who found out through ultrasound testing that they were expecting a girl had abortions. There were also cases of infanticide: girl babies being killed immediately after birth so families could try to have a boy. As a result of abortion and infanticide, by 1993 the ratio of male to female births in China was unnaturally skewed in favor of males. More than 12 percent of all female fetuses were being aborted or had otherwise disappeared.

Another problem the regime faced was separatism among China's non-Chinese minorities. Only under the Manchus were China's borders as extensive as under the Communists, and in the 1980s and early 1990s some of the vast outlying areas were becoming increasingly restive. The northwestern territory of Xinjiang, an area four times the size of California, is inhabited mainly by 16 million Muslims of Turkic origin. They resent Chinese control, and their hopes of breaking away from Beijing grew after the collapse of the Soviet Union and the rise of newly independent Muslim states in neighboring Central Asia.

Opposition to Chinese control was also strong in Tibet, the home of a people with a Buddhist culture that dates back over 1,200 years. For the Tibetans, whose revolt against Beijing was brutally suppressed in 1959, Chinese rule since 1950 has been a catastrophe. It has, in fact, amounted to genocide. As many as 1.2 million Tibetans—about one fifth of the population—have died under Chinese rule. Only 13 out of 6,000 monasteries survived the Cultural Revolution, while 60 percent of Tibet's sacred scrolls, religious texts, and books have been destroyed since 1950. And Chinese immigration into Tibet has turned the Tibetans into a minority in their own country. But harsh repression could not extinguish the resistance of the Tibetan people, who staged repeated demonstrations.

China's relationship with the world outside its borders reflected its growing military as well as economic power. By the 1990s it was the world's fifth largest arms exporter. Some of these exports aroused international concern because China was selling extremely destructive weapons and technology to aggressive and unstable nations. The transactions included nuclear technology and chemical weapons for Iran, one of the most aggressive countries in the Middle East, and advanced weapons for Saudi Arabia and Syria. Other controversial Chinese exports were products produced in the *laogoi* prison camp factories and sold to foreigners who were not aware of the products' origin. The United States was one country concerned that it might unknowingly be importing goods produced by Chinese slave laborers.

Worshipers were allowed to return to this Chinese
Buddhist temple in the mid-1980s. Although the
government has relaxed some restrictions on religion
and commerce, it has permitted little political dissent.

Closer to home, China's modernization and buildup of its own military forces disturbed several of its neighbors, including Japan, India, Vietnam, and several smaller countries in Southeast Asia. Ironically, the PRC's relations with Taiwan steadily improved, despite Beijing's continued claim that the Nationalist-controlled island legally belonged to the PRC. Taiwanese investment in China and trade between Taiwan and the PRC boomed. The two countries also signed agreements in April 1993 concerning matters such as communication and cooperation against crime.

Politics was the area in which the least change took place during the early 1990s. Although officially retired as of 1990, eighty-nine-year-old Deng Xiaoping remained in charge in China. He and a small group of aged veterans of the pre-1949 era still made the country's most important decisions. Among the younger generation of leaders, Prime Minister Li Peng appeared to be the most powerful, but his health was questionable and he was widely hated for his role in the Tiananmen Square massacre. Other younger politicians were jockeying for power, and it was generally agreed that China could face political instability when Deng finally passed from the scene.

The Search for China's Soul

Almost a century ago, as China's ancient Confucian world crumbled around him and no viable alternative to it seemed in sight, a Chinese reformer named Liang Qichiao asked, "Oh, where now is the soul of China?" That question haunted China's intellectuals for the next half century as China staggered from one crisis to another. For a short time after 1949 it appeared that Mao Zedong and the Chinese Communist party might provide the answer. But the Great Leap Forward and the Cultural Revolution shattered whatever faith most Chinese had in Maoism-Marxism. And while after 1978 Deng Xiaoping brought impressive economic growth to China, his economic policies discredited rather than reinforced Marxism. Nor was Deng's emphasis on material progress—while totally rejecting Western democratic values—a substitute for the worldviews provided by Confucianism and Marxism. As one expert on China observed:

> By the 1990s, Marxism-Maoism has fallen even lower than Confucianism in popular acceptance. Yet, while ideologies have slipped out of daily life, the space they have left remains and begs to be filled. Here and there one can observe signs of continued Chinese yearning for a distinctive moral-social-political core.[13]

One reason China in the early 1990s seemed consumed by the race to get rich was that the future was so uncertain. Would Deng's passing lead to another drastic change of direction? Would people have any time to enjoy what they had acquired? Uncertainty and the lack of any moral focus in Deng's China produced a renewed interest in Confucianism as well as a religious revival in which many Chinese turned to Buddhism and Christianity. After forty-four years of Communist

13. Perry Link, "China's 'Core' Problem," in *Daedalus*, vol. 122, no. 2 (Spring 1993), p. 196.

rule, China was still wandering between two worlds, this time the failed world of communism and a post-Communist world as yet not born. This condition may have raised in the minds of millions of Chinese the same question about Mao's revolution that the English poet Matthew Arnold asked about earlier struggles to change the world:

> For what availed it, all the noise
> And outcry of the former men?
> Say, have their sons achieved more joys,
> Say, is life lighter now than then?
> The sufferers died, they left their pain—
> The pangs that tortured them remain.[14]

14. Matthew Arnold, "Tales from the Grand Chartreuse," *The Poems of Matthew Arnold*, ed. Kenneth Allott (New York: Barnes and Noble, 1965), p. 291.

GLOSSARY

alchemy: medieval chemistry in which the goal was to change ordinary metals into gold.

Bolshevism: the ideology or beliefs of radical Russian Marxists who seized control of Russia in 1917 and established a totalitarian dictatorship.

bourgeois: belonging to the middle class. To Marxists, the bourgeois class was the dominant class in the capitalist system. Hence, to refer to someone as "bourgeois," as Mao often did to party rivals who disagreed with him, was to portray them as enemies of the revolution.

calligraphy: the art of beautiful handwriting. It was highly developed and considered an art form in traditional China.

capitalism: an economic system in which investment in and ownership of production is in private hands. Marxists consider capitalism the last economic stage before socialism. They say that capitalism, and the bourgeoisie that is the dominant class under capitalism, must be overthrown in a revolution before socialism can be established.

collectivization: the process of taking the land of private farmers and combining that land into large cooperatively worked farms called "collective farms." This process was done with great violence and destruction in the Soviet Union in the 1930s. The Chinese Communist party under Mao completed the job of collectivization with less violence during the 1950s.

Confucianism: the ethical belief system of traditional China that valued above all else an orderly society in which each person knew and accepted his designated place.

counterrevolutionary: someone who wants to reverse a revolution. The charge of being counterrevolutionary is one of the gravest that one Marxist can make against another.

despotism: a government in which the ruler holds absolute power.

dynasty: a series of rulers from the same family or group.

fascism: a dictatorial political and social system emphasizing aggressive and extreme nationalism and often racism.

First United Front: the Soviet-sponsored political alliance formed between the Chinese Communist party and the Guomindang that lasted from 1923 to 1927.

five-year plan: a strategy for government-directed development along socialist lines. First developed and used in the Soviet Union and later adopted by the People's Republic of China.

Gang of Four: a political faction formed and led by Mao's wife, Jiang Qing, that was defeated in the struggle for power after Mao's death.

Great Leap Forward: Mao's policy in the late 1950s and early 1960s for moving directly to communism. It ended in disastrous failure and caused a terrible famine.

Great Proletarian Cultural Revolution: Mao's policy for completely overhauling Chinese culture of the mid- and late-

1960s. The aim was to root out all capitalist, bourgeois, and nonsocialist tendencies in China, as defined by Mao. This led to chaos and destruction on a mass scale. More commonly referred to as simply the Cultural Revolution.

Guomindang: the Nationalist party in China. First led by Sun Yatsen and later by Chiang Kai-shek.

hierarchical: ranking one person or group above another.

laogoi: the network of prison camps in Communist China. It is still in existence today.

Leninism: the ideas of Vladimir Lenin, the founder and leader of the Marxist Bolshevik party in Russia. The Chinese Communist party considers itself Marxist-Leninist.

li: the Confucian concept of behavior according to status. Under *li*, people are expected to behave according to strict rules that apply to their social status in society.

Little Red Book: the collection of Mao's quotations that was carried around and constantly read by millions of Chinese during the Cultural Revolution.

loess: the fine, easily worked soil of northern China.

Long March: the Communist party's escape from Chiang Kai-shek's forces during 1934–1935 in which the CCP, enduring terrible hardships, marched 6,000 miles (9,650 kilometers) in little over a year. Although a defeat in the short run, the Long March marked the rebirth of the CCP under Mao's leadership.

Manchukuo: the name of the Japanese puppet state set up in Manchuria after the Japanese occupied the region in 1931.

Maoism: Mao's version of Marxism, which blended traditional Marxism with several of Mao's own ideas.

Marxism: a doctrine based on the ideas of Karl Marx that says the victory of socialism over capitalism is inevitable. The Chinese Communist party is a Marxist party.

mass line: Mao's doctrine that the Chinese Communist party had to listen to the peasantry and share the hardships of their lives before it could expect to lead them toward a genuine socialist revolution.

nationalism: devotion to the interests of one's own nation.

People's Communes: the gigantic communal institutions in the countryside established during the Great Leap Forward; these were to be the basis of China's conversion to communism.

People's Liberation Army (PLA): The army of the Chinese Communist party. Prior to 1946 known as the Red Army.

pi: the Greek letter used as the symbol for the ratio between the circumference and diameter of a circle.

proletariat: the working class under capitalism. According to traditional Marxism, the working class, or proletariat, will rise up to overthrow capitalism and establish socialism. One of Mao's major changes in Marxism is that he substituted the peasantry for the proletariat in his revolutionary scheme.

propaganda: information or ideas systematically spread to further or hinder a cause, nation, person, etc. From the point of view of Communist parties, propaganda is spreading the party's message to a large number of people.

Red Guard: Millions of fanatical teenage supporters of Mao during the Cultural Revolution. The Red Guards were responsible for countless acts of destruction and violence between 1966 and 1969.

renaissance: a vigorous revival or rebirth of a society or culture.

republic: a country in which power rests in the body of citizens who are entitled to vote and who select representatives to exercise that power.

revisionism: in Marxism, the act of revising Marx's ideas. Revisionism was considered a sin in both the Bolshevik party and the Chinese Communist party, and Mao often attacked his opponents within the party by calling them revisionists.

rightists: those who were critical of Mao and the Chinese Communist party just before and during the Great Leap Forward. After the GLF the term continued to be used against those who disagreed with Mao.

scientific method: the method of scientific inquiry developed in Europe during the seventeenth century that led to the Scientific Revolution.

Second United Front: the uneasy alliance for the purpose of resisting the Japanese invasion of China between the Chinese Communist party and the Guomindang from 1937 until the end of World War II.

socialism: the theory and system of social organization that advocates ownership of society's wealth by the community as a whole. According to socialism, society should be organized on a cooperative rather than a competitive basis.

Stalinism: the version of Marxism associated with Joseph Stalin, the dictator of the Soviet Union between 1929 and 1953. Stalinism also refers to the Soviet economic, political, and social system that was built in the Soviet Union during the Stalin era.

warlords: military leaders who controlled areas of China from about 1916 until the late 1920s, when the central government was in a state of collapse. Some of them retained a large degree of control over certain areas even after the Guomindang under Chiang established itself as the government of China.

zhengfeng: Mao's system of indoctrination of party cadres that was used with great success during the Yan'an era.

RECOMMENDED READING

Buchanan, Keith, Charles P. Fitzgerald, and Colin A. Ronan. *China: The Land and the People*. New York: Crown Publishers, 1980.

Clayre, Alasdair. *The Heart of the Dragon*. Boston: Houghton Mifflin, 1984.

Dawson, Raymond. *The Chinese Experience*. New York: Scribner, 1978.

Fairbank, John King. *The Great Chinese Revolution*. New York: Harper & Row, 1986.

Hsü, Immanuel C. Y. *China Without Mao: The Search for a New Order*. 2d ed. New York and Oxford: Oxford University Press, 1990.

Hsü, Immanuel C. Y. *The Rise of Modern China*. 4th ed. New York and Oxford: Oxford University Press, 1990.

Liang Heng and Judith Shapiro. *Son of the Revolution*. New York: Random House, 1983.

Mao Zedong. *Chairman Mao Talks to the People: Talks and Letters, 1956–1971*. Stuart Schram, ed. New York: Pantheon, 1974.

Meisner, Maurice. *Mao's China and After*. New York: The Free Press, 1986.

Rice, Edgar. *Mao's Way*. Berkeley: University of California Press, 1972.

Shen Tong. *Almost a Revolution*. Boston: Houghton Mifflin, 1990.

Snow, Edgar. *Red Star Over China*, rev. and enlarged ed. New York: Grove Press, 1968.

Spence, Jonathan D. *The Search for Modern China*. New York: Norton, 1990.

Uhalley, Stephen, Jr. *A History of the Chinese Communist Party*. Stanford, Calif.: Hoover Institution Press, 1988.

INDEX

Page numbers in *italics* refer to illustrations.

ABOUT THE AUTHOR

Michael G. Kort's previous books
for young readers include
The Cold War and *Marxism in Power*,
both from The Millbrook Press,
as well as biographies of
Soviet leaders Nikita Khrushchev
and Mikhail Gorbachev and
several histories of the Soviet Union.

He is also coauthor of a college text-
book on twentieth-century China,
Modernization and Revolution in China.

A professor of social science at
Boston University, he lives
in Brookline, Massachusetts.